DATE DUE		
MAY -6 '94		
DEC 27 '94		
JUL 29 2005		

SHERIFF
PAT GARRETT'S
LAST DAYS

Colin Rickards

Sunstone Press
Santa Fe, New Mexico

First Edition

Printed in the United States of America

Library of Congress Cataloging in Publication Data:

Rickards, Colin.
    Sheriff Pat Garrett's last days.

    Bibliography p. 92.
    Includes index.
    1. Garrett, Pat F. (Pat Floyd), 1850-1908--Assassi-
nation. 2. Sheriffs--New Mexico--Biography. 3. New
Mexico--Biography. 4. Frontier and pioneer life--New
Mexico. 5. New Mexico--History--1848-   . I. Title.
F801.G3R53   1986   978.9'04'0924 [B]   85-25020
ISBN 0-86534-079-X

Published in 1986 by SUNSTONE PRESS
            Post Office Box 2321
            Santa Fe, NM 87504-2321 / USA

CONTENTS

"He was a good Sheriff at a time when New Mexico needed just such a man" – Jim East, former Sheriff of Oldham County, Texas, to Eugene Manlove Rhodes.

"Naturally Garrett had enemies – all men of prominence have . . . A man of the law is naturally hated by the lawless, and this famous hunter of desperadoes knew that he was both feared and hated by this class and their sympathizers" John M. Scanland in **Life of Pat F. Garrett**, 1908.

"He was a tall, spare man, with noticeably long legs and arms. He was a silent man, but nevertheless pleasant to talk with. Coolness, courage, and determination were written on his face" – Albert E. Hyde, **Century Magazine**, March, 1902.

AUTHOR'S NOTE

Many people have helped me in the digging out of what I believe to be the true story of the events leading up to and surrounding the death of Patrick Floyd Garrett. In a few cases, because this unhappy affair still remains a source of controversy more than sixty years after it occurred, old-timers — wishing to help for the sake of history, but unwilling to become engaged in acrimonious discussion in their twilight years — have asked that their contributions remain anonymous, a restriction which I regret but understand and to which I have adhered. My thanks to them for sharing confidences.

Others who have assisted in this work, in alphabetical order, are accorded my thanks, too.

Jeffrey Burton, of London, England, friend and author, generously took time off from his own researches to read the manuscript and make helpful suggestions; Max M. Coleman, of Lubbock, Texas, contributed reminiscences of his own dealings with "Killing Jim" Miller; Phil Cooke, owner-publisher of **The Press of the Territorian,** at Santa Fe, New Mexico, gave me the hospitality of his home, and encouragement and assistance long-range in running down various leads; Hiram M. Dow, of Mayhill, New Mexico, told me much about his distinguished peace officer father, J. Les Dow; Allen A. Erwin, of Desert Hot Springs, California, provided me with information he had collected about the activities of Jim Miller; W.H. Hutchinson, of Chico, California, author and authority on old-time New Mexico and especially on the life, times and writings of Eugene Manlove Rhodes, kindly gave invaluable guidance along a tangled trail; William A. Keleher, author, attorney and historian, of Albuquerque, New Mexico, provided clues, gave advice and permitted me the use of some of his frontier photographs; Judge James B. McGhee, of Santa Fe, New Mexico, provided reminiscences about people — especially lawyers — and places which were exceptionally helpful; Fred Mazzulla, of Denver, Colorado, author and Westerner, as well as owner of the largest private collection of Western photographs in the world, supplied a useful piece of information; Leon Claire Metz, of El Paso, Texas, author and authority on the life and times of Pat Garrett, read and criticized the final manuscript; Robert N. Mullin, of South Laguna, California, without doubt one of the most knowledgeable of writers and historians on the Southwest, read the manuscript, offered constant encouragement and provided such material on Wayne Brazel and other personalities; Lee Myers, of Carlsbad, New Mexico, author and researcher, helped with some valuable material on Les Dow; Miss Alberta Pantle, former Librarian of the Kansas State Historical Society, and a valued guide and friend for a number years, aided in researching the activities of the Brazel family in Kansas; Perry J. Sherman, of Corpus Christi, Texas, related his memories of Jim Miller's execution at the hands of vigilantes in Oklahoma and clinched two vital points; William R. Smith, of Liverpool, England, authority on the literature of the Southwest, especially that relating to the fictional treatments of the Fountain and Garrett cases, generously provided guide notes from his own researches and willingly criticized the final manuscript; Clarence Snook, of Lebanon, Ohio, supplied his reminiscences as the driver of the spring-wagon which carried Garrett's body from the scene of the murder to Las Cruces; and Dr. C.L. Sonnichsen, of El Paso, Texas, whose friendship and encouragement in various projects over the years has been a constant source of inspiration, and whose own contribution to the written history of the Southwest has been outstanding, assisted immeasurably, and his own writings on feuds in Texas and the Tularosa country were a guide.

Finally, my thanks to the staff members of the following institutions, whose resources and collections were exceptionally useful: the British Museum Reading Room, London, England; the Southwest Room, El Paso Public Library, El Paso, Texas; the American History Room, New York Public Library, New York; the Arizona Pioneers' Historical Society, Tucson, Arizona; Division of Manuscripts, University of Oklahoma, Norman, Oklahoma; The Museum of New Mexico, Santa Fe, New Mexico; and the New Mexico State Library, Santa Fe.

To all those who helped I express my gratitude. Conclusions drawn by me, and statements made herein are, of course, my own responsibility.

Colin Rickards,
London England

CHAPTER 1
THE MAN WHO HAD TO DIE

Pat Garrett has been maligned by writers, libelled by Hollywood and deprecated by many of his contemporaries, but despite them all his deeds retain for him a niche in the gallery of fast shooting peace officers who helped to bring law and order to the frontier West. When he died there was rejoicing in some quarters and relief in others — as might be expected in the case of a controversial figure — but there was also genuine and profound sorrow in the rugged hearts of many in New Mexico, Texas and Arizona, as well as farther afield, and the circumstances surrounding his death, ostensibly at the hands of a most unlikely cowboy named Wayne Brazel, have puzzled and intrigued historians since that spring day in 1908 when he was shot to death and left lying in a sand drift on a lonely road.

Patrick Floyd Garrett was born in Chambers County, Alabama, on 5th June, 1850, and grew up in Claiborne Parish, Louisiana. His father, Colonel John L. Garrett, had a prosperous plantation and raised six children.[1] Young Pat went to Lancaster in Dallas County, Texas, in 1869 and worked there as a cowboy until 1875, when he quit a Kansas-bound trail herd to become a buffalo hunter in the employ of W. Skelton Glenn. Garrett, who subsequently became a junior partner in Glenn's outfit, hunted in the Texas Panhandle for something less than three years, killing a young Irishman named Joe Briscoe after a verbal clash turned into a physical dispute with blows being struck and ended with Garrett going to his bedroll to get his pistol. By his own account he reported the matter to the authorities at Fort Griffin, but found them disinclined to take any action.[2] In mid-February, 1878, Garrett rode into Fort Sumner,[3] New Mexico, with Glenn and Nick Ross. When the other two returned to Texas he stayed behind, took a job working cattle for Pete Maxwell, and, perhaps surprisingly, managed to stay out of the mopping-up operations which took place in the wake of the so-called Lincoln County War,[4] a rangeland flare-up to decide which of two factions would control Lincoln County financially and politically. He married Juanita Gutierrez, but she died shortly after the wedding and on 14th January, 1880, Pat Garrett married her sister Polinaria at the town of Anton Chico.[5] In time, they produced eight children.

On 7th November the same year, with the backing of prominent members of the local "reform faction," Garrett was elected Sheriff of Lincoln County, with the prime task of running down the notorious Billy the Kid[6] and putting him, along with his rustler band, out of business, one way or another. The man he defeated in the election, George Kimbrell, resigned and Garrett was appointed to see out the last two months of Kimbrell's office. On the night of 19th/20th December, at Fort Sumner, Garrett's gun was one of two which ended the life of Tom O'Folliard,[7] the Kid's friend and companion, and a few days later his posse captured the Kid, Dave Rudabaugh,[8] Billy Wilson[9] and Tom Pickett[10] at Stinking Springs. Charlie Bowdre[11] was killed there in a blast of gunfire, the shooting being done by Garrett and six other men. After the Kid's trial and escape, Garrett, John W. Poe[12] and Thomas L. "Tip" McKinney tracked him to Fort Sumner and on the night of 14th July, 1881, Garrett killed him in Pete Maxwell's house.[13] Garrett got the $500 reward money but was not re-elected for a second term as Sheriff of Lincoln County. He bought and operated a small livestock ranch at Eagle Creek — near where incidentally, the father of Wayne Brazel who later confessed to killing Garrett, filed a claim when he first arrived in New Mexico — and soon afterwards began work on a book about Billy the Kid.[14]

The mawkish interest in Western outlaws exhibited by the Eastern reading public spawned a whole flood of lurid little volumes. Pat Garrett's avowed intention in writing **The Authentic Life of Billy, the Kid** was to present the truth about the young outlaw, though he undoubtedly also hoped to vindicate himself and to cash in on the boom in such works. By the time that Garrett got his book out in April, 1882, a total of eight so-called "biographies" of Billy the Kid had already appeared and Garrett's was not a financial success.[15] A little less than two years later he received a commission from Governor John Ireland of Texas to organize a Texas Ranger company in the Panhandle country. He sold his ranch to Captain Brandon Kirby — a haughty Englishman who called his ranch hands "cowservants" — and moved to Texas. His Rangers, whose pay was guaranteed by the large stockmen of the region, operated with some degree of success against rustlers and Garrett renewed his acquaintance with a number of prominent men, the majority of whom thought highly of him.[16] He soon became one of the best-known men in the Southwest. Resigning his Ranger commission after rather less than three years, he returned to New Mexico and managed his old ranch for Kirby and his partner Charles Cree, a retired whisky distiller from Scotland. Then, in 1887, he branched out on his own and moved to Roswell. When Chaves County was carved out of the old Lincoln County in 1889 he decided to run for Sheriff, but was beaten by a man backed by his old deputy, John W. Poe. Garrett's son Jarvis said later that his father was "disgruntled and bitter"[17] about losing the election and in October the same year he left his wife and family to operate their ranch near Roswell and went to Uvalde, Texas, where, in due course, he became a county commissioner, settled his family and began work anew. Garrett was popular in Uvalde and it was a happy time for his family, although originally they had opposed the move from New Mexico. He had a weakness for gambling, however, and much of the money he made raising and breeding quarter horses and thoroughbreds was lost betting on them, and other people's animals, at the tracks.[18]

Part of Garrett's trouble was that he was restless, as well as financially hard-pressed, and when Governor William T. Thornton of New Mexico offered him $150 a month, and a chance at a reward of $8,000, to take charge of a particularly unpleasant murder investigation he jumped at the opportunity. The post of Sheriff of Dona Ana County, vacated by the incumbent but unexpired, was thrown in and Garrett changed political parties to accept it. There seemed to be a strong possiblity of his winning the election at the polls, and, with the job being worth $6,000 a year, he felt that he had made a move which would enable him to get out of his financial troubles and give his family a better life.[19]

The murder investigation in question concerned the disappearance of Colonel Albert Jennings Fountain and his eight-year-old son Henry at Chalk Hill, just west of White Sands, on the Tularosa road, on or about 1st February, 1896. Fountain was a controversial man, an adventurer with a Quixotic mentality and a flair for personal publicity, a frontier lawyer and newspaper editor, an Indian fighter and, latterly, either a fiercely-hated or much-loved politician, depending upon which party's supporters spoke of him. He was in possession of indictments charging cattle larceny and brand defacing by Oliver Lee[20] and William McNew,[21] among others, at the time of his disappearance, indictments which had been drawn up on evidence presented by stock detective J. Les Dow, an able and efficient range man and frontier peace officer. The questions of exactly what happened to Fountain and his young son that day, who killed them, how, and where they were buried, have never been adequately answered and the double murder is still New Mexico's most debated crime. It is impossible to overstate either the bitterness which was stirred up in the Territory by the disappearance of Fountain and his son, or the deep-rooted determination of the guilty parties to stop at nothing to protect themselves from detection.[22]

Pat Garrett made it fairly clear from the beginning that he intended to work the case out for himself. He was less than helpful to Pinkerton operative J.C. Fraser who was assigned to the case and his obvious determination to obtain evidence to convict Oliver Lee, William McNew and Jim Gililland[23] quickly brought the enmity of the men. He seemed to see himself as a one-man avenging force, accepted neither advice nor guidance and eventually obtained bench warrants for the arrest of his suspects.[24] McNew was detained but the other two men, especially Lee, were reluctant to surrender to Garrett as it was bruited about that the Sheriff intended to shoot first and serve his warrants afterwards.[25] Les Dow was already dead. Fresh from hunting the "Black Jack" Christian[26] gang in the western part of New Mexico, he had returned to Eddy to take up the post of Sheriff of Eddy County and seven weeks later been shot down by a ne'er-do-well named Dave Kemp, who managed to escape a conviction for murder.[27] There is no doubt that Garrett's life, too, was in considerable danger because of the hunt for Oliver Lee and Jim Gililland, and it may well have been this factor which caused itchy trigger fingers when Garrett and a posse raided Lee's ranch at Wildey Well during the night of 12th July, 1898. Shots were fired at sleeping men as the posse arrived, confirming Lee's belief that he was not to be taken alive, but the attack was a failure and cost the life of Deputy Sheriff Kent Kearney. The wanted men got away.[28] After some unprecedented juggling by politicians, including the creation of a completely new county, Oliver Lee and Jim Gililland surrendered, though not to Garrett, and faced trial. The mercurial Albert Bacon Fall[29] appeared for the defendants Lee and Gililland. The eighteen-day court hearing at Hillsboro — during May and June, 1899 — was very much a political trial of strength as Fall tangled with his arch foe Thomas Benton Catron,[30] leader of the influential — some said politically and financially corrupt — "Santa Fe Ring," who appeared as a Special Prosecutor for the Territory.

The accused men were acquitted in this trial, which in a real sense became more of a political slugging match between Fall and Catron. Pat Garrett, way out of his class when these bitter old rivals went to war against each other was, ultimately, the real loser. Whether Oliver Lee himself actually participated in the killing of Fountain and his son, or was merely guilty by prior knowledge and collusion, has never been shown to any satisfactory degree.[31]

In the first few days of October, 1899, Pat Garrett, who by this time had secured election as Sheriff of Dona Ana County, learned that a young man named Reed was working at the San Augustine Ranch at Organ Gap, owned by W.W. Cox, doughty Texan fighter and brother-in-law of Oliver Lee. On 7th October, accompanied by a Deputy named Jose Espalin — who had been with him at the Wildey Well fight — and Sheriff Blaylock of Greer County, Oklahoma, Garrett rode out to the ranch to find out if Reed was in fact one Norman Newman, wanted for killing his partner in Sheriff Blaylock's baliwick eleven months before. The accounts of those present indicate that there was more than a reasonable charge of taking the man alive, but Reed was killed after a gunfight which started in the kitchen where he was helping the pregnant Mrs. Cox with the washing up. Not surprisingly, she had a miscarriage as a result of the incident and Garrett thus incurred the hatred of W.W. Cox. Officially, it was recorded that Espalin had fired the fatal bullet. The body was taken back to Oklahoma for identification and the reward was claimed. It was never paid, however, providing interesting gossip for New Mexicans, who decided that this meant that the pleasant boy who called himself Reed was not the fugitive murderer Norman Newman.[32]

After the expiration of his term as Sheriff of Dona Ana County — he failed to get re-elected — Garrett went into the livery stable business in Las Cruces, and some two years later became Collector of Customs at El Paso, Texas. His appointment, effective from 20th December, 1901, was made by President Theodore Roosevelt,[33] former Rough Rider in the Spanish-American War, national hero and a great admirer of Western lawmen of the Pat Garrett stamp. Roosevelt was a little worried at the flood of telegrams which reached him protesting the choice of applicant,[34] for Pat Garrett was building up for himself a formidable array of enemies, but there were congratulations, too. He served faithfully, if not without criticism,[35] for four years but was not re-appointed, his term expiring on New Year's Day, 1906.

Pat Garrett's friend John Nance Garner, "Cactus Jack," destined to become Vice-President of the United States, knew of Pat's prediliction for poker and also that he was openhanded to all when he had money, which was why he seldom had any. When Garner wrote from Uvalde to congratulate Garrett on his new post as Collector of Customs, he remarked: "All your friends in this place are jubilant over your appointment, and, of course, expect you to make a barrel of money. Of course, I join in their views and jubilation, but I do not tell them that I am confident that at the end of your term of office, you won't have a cent more than you have now. Because in a big game, I suppose you could lose a year's salary or in two or three sittings; and you always imagined you could play poker." He knew the kind of big stakes poker games that went on in El Paso, sometimes lasting for ninety-six hours non-stop. He also knew Pat Garrett's tendency towards speculations, some of them in land, and advised him against such ventures.[36]

"John Garner's prediction to the effect that Garrett would not have a cent more at the end of his term as Collector of Customs was amazingly accurate," wrote Jarvis P. Garrett, the lawman's son. "In fact, if anything, he had less. Apart from that, his signature appeared on a note, as co-signer, to an Albuquerque bank, under which George Curry had borrowed three thousand dollars."[37]

Curry[38] was serving as the civil governor of a province in the

Philippine Islands, captured from Spain in the Spanish-American War of 1898, when the note became due.

"The bank considered it would be too troublesome to sue him for the amount owed, and even if judgement could be obtained in the Philippines, it was doubtful they could collect since his only income was that received as salary from the government," Jarvis Garrett added. "Consequently, action was taken against Garrett to cover Curry's indebtedness."[39]

It was a severe blow and plunged Pat Garrett into financial difficulties from which he never recovered. To meet the demand by the Albuquerque bankers he mortgaged all his land, except for a ranch at Bear Canyon and the piece on which his home stood, to a merchant in Las Cruces for the sum of $3,000 and cleared Curry's debt.[40] It was a short-term transaction, as the merchant needed repayment within a given time, and Garrett was sure that his friendship with Curry would enable him to collect the debt. In April, 1907, when Curry was appointed Governor of New Mexico, things looked brighter, but Garrett's hopes were soon dashed. Curry did not have the money. It seems he agreed to pay the debt off gradually. The merchant apparently consented to take only $2,000 in repayment, though whether this was to clear the loan completely is unsure and it may be that Garrett was to lose part of his land to cover the other $1,000, or else was to pay it off on a time basis. Whatever the agreement, the sum of $2,000 had to be raised at once to repay the lender and Garrett approached W.H.H. Llewellyn,[41] a mutual friend, to tackle George Curry on his behalf.[42] Again, the cash was not forthcoming and Garrett was in further trouble. He was also being dunned for several years' back taxes which added to his difficulties. Eventually he managed to negotiate a loan of $3,500 from his neighbor, W.W. Cox, hoping that the sum would cover both the $2,000 owed to the merchant and his own delinquent taxes.[43]

In the last years of his life — especially the last two financially-troubled years — Pat Garrett became increasingly, and perhaps understandably, morose. He drank heavily, gambled daringly — and mostly unsuccessfully — in an attempt to get out of his money troubles, and became argumentative and overbearing. There is no doubt that people were afraid of his temper, and liquor did not mellow him. On the contrary, it made him more aggressive and even more sure and swift in his reflex actions. A story got around that he had pistol-whipped a neighboring rancher on one occasion and, on what turned out to his final visit to El Paso, he received an anonymous letter containing a threat of death.[44] The tough "sporting men" of El Paso walked warily when Garrett was in town, and even his long-time friend Tom Powers, the one-eyed owner of the "Coney Island" Saloon — once described as the resort of "all the uncaged convicts in the West" — was careful to humor him when he saw the signs of trouble. Garrett had taken Powers to the "Rough Rider's convention" at San Antonio in 1905 and had gratified the man's ambition to meet President Roosevelt, who was there as guest of honor.[45] Garrett and Powers were friends, close friends, but Powers was a cautious man, used to trouble and readily able to size up Garrett when the danger signs appeared.

The time he spent in Uvalde must, in retrospect, have seemed to Garrett to have been his golden years. True, he was as always financially hard-pressed, but he was also liked and respected and if he had remained there his life might have been less frustrating and more fruitful and secure. Even so, during 1906-07, overburdened with money worries as he was, Pat Garrett fought back manfully.

"Beginning on a shoestring with what little he could muster and borrow, Garrett decided to acquire some brood mares and stallions to start breeding and raising quarter horses, in the hope that this time the wheels of fortune would favor him," his son Jarvis wrote.[46]

The ranch was on the Eastern slopes of the San Andres, a four hour drive from Las Cruces.

He had, however, unwittingly delivered himself into the hands of his enemies and they showed him no mercy. The day was not far off when he would die with a bullet in the back of his head and another in his belly out along the Las Cruces road.

NOTES
CHAPTER 1

1. For biographical sketches of Pat Garrett's career — the two biographies of him make scant pretence at scholarship — see **The Fabulous Frontier: Twelve New Mexico Items** by William A. Keleher (The Rydal Press, Santa Fe, 1945, used in this study; reprinted 1962), pp. 57 -82; **Tularosa: Last of the Frontier West** by C.L. Sonnichsen (Devin-Adair, New York, 1961), pp. 228-44; "Pat Garrett — Two Forgotten Killings" by Robert N. Mullin (**Password**, El Paso County Historical Society, 1965), pp. 57-62; "A Pat Garrett Item" by Philip J. Rasch (**New Mexco Historical Review,** Volume XXXII, January, 1961), pp. 80-82; "Pat Garrett and His Book" by J.C. Dykes, which was published as the Introduction to **The Authentic Life of Billy, the Kid** by Patrick Floyd Garrett (University of Oklahoma Press edition, Norman, 1954), pp. xi-xxviii; and "Foreword" by Jarvis P. Garrett, son of Pat Garrett, included in a later edition of the above mentioned book, (Horn and Wallace, Albuquerque, 1964), pp. 7-49.
2. "Two Forgotten Killings," Mullin art. cit., pp. 57-59. Mr. Mullin's account is based on W. Skelton Glenn's reminiscences; see also "The Recollections of W.S. Glenn, Buffalo Hunter" (Ed.) Rex W. Strickland (**Panhandle-Plains Historical Review,** Canyon, Volume XXIII, 1949), pp. 15-83. W.H. Sanders also witnessed the killing of Briscoe and said later that it was done "with little or no provocation" — **Another Verdict for Oliver Lee** by W.H. Hutchinson (Clarendon Press, Clarendon, Texas, 1965), p. 10. Hutchinson quotes extensively from letters written to him by an old range rider who was in a position to know much but asked not be identified. He calls his informant the "Cowman," following, he explains, "a convention sanctified by Stewart Edward White," who in his excellent collection of range tales, **Arizona Nights** (Doubleday, Page & Co., New York, 1913) spoke many truths through the lips of a character called "The Cattleman." The noted Western writer Emerson Hough, who was Garrett's friend for many years, wrote that Garrett "rarely spoke" about Briscoe's death — "indeed he never mentioned it to me until some twenty years after I first knew him." It was Hough's contention that the killing affected Garrett and played on his mind for much of his life — "Travelling the Old Trails" by Emerson Hough (**Saturday Evening Post,** 4th October, 1919). Sonnichsen, **Tularosa,** op. cit., 232, says that the man Garrett killed was Skelton Glenn. He cites John Meadows in the Alamogordo **News,** 8th March, 1936, but Meadows was mistaken. Glenn lived until the mid-1920s.
3. Jarvis P. Garrett, op. cit., p. 13, Keleher, **Fabulous Frontier,** op. cit., p. 58, and Sonnichsen, **Tularosa,** op. cit., p. 233, say that Garrett arrived in Fort Sumner in the fall of 1878, but Mullin, op. cit., p. 59, working from W. Skelton Glenn's manuscript, says that it was "in mid-February (1878)" that

Garrett, Glenn and Nick Ross rode from their base at Casas Amarillas in Texas, north and west to the settlement of Taiban, New Mexico, and from there to Fort Sumner, arriving towards the end of the month. In his excellent short work **A Chronology of the Lincoln County War** (Press of the Territorian, Santa Fe, 1966), p. 19, Mullin lists late February for Garrett's arrival in Fort Sumner. Further evidence of a spring rather than a fall arrival is provided by Charles Ballard, early-day rancher and peace officer, who remarks that his father, A.J. Ballard, also a buffalo hunter in the Casas Amarillas country, moved the whole family westward early in 1878, passing through Fort Griffin on the way to Fort Sumner "in February" and arrived at their destination "after about three weeks travelling." He adds: "Pat Garrett was working for a cow outfit there. He had reached there just a few days before" — **Charles Littlepage Ballard** — **Southwesterner** by Colin Rickards ("Southwestern Studies," Volume IV, Number 4, Texas Western Press, El Paso, 1966), pp. 6-8.

4. The Lincoln County War began in earnest on 18th February, 1878, with the murder of John H. Tunstall by a posse, and ended — except for a few sporadic outbursts of violence — with the fight in Lincoln between the rival factions of the Murphy-Riley-Dolan business interests and those of Chisum-McSween. It was virtually the last act in the "War" and took place during mid-July, 1878. For a detailed account of this fight, drawn from original sources, see "Five Days of Battle" by Philip J. Rasch (Denver Westerners' **Brand Book**, Volume II, 1956), pp. 294-323. A comprehensive account of the "troubles" is contained in **Violence in Lincoln County, 1869-1881** by William A. Keleher (University of New Mexico Press, Albuquerque, 1957). An excellent brief sketch is "War in Lincoln County" by Philip J. Rasch (English Westerners' **Brand Book**, Volume 6, Number 4, July, 1964), pp. 2-11. Rasch has specialized in the affairs of the area at this period and has published in various places a vast body of documented work. Also of value, though undocumented, is "How the Lincoln County War Started" by Philip J. Rasch (**True West**, Austin, Volume 9, Number 4, Whole Number 50, March-April, 1962), p. 30 et seq. Extensive coverage of the opening shots will be found in "Prelude to War in Lincoln County: The Murder of John H. Tunstall" by Philip J. Rasch (Denver Westerners' **Brand book**, Volume 7, 1957) pp. 78-96. Other recent works of scholarship dealing with the "troubles" are **The Life and Death of John Henry Tunstall** by Frederick W. Nolan (University of New Mexico Press, Albuquerque, 1965), and **Maurice Garland Fulton's History of the Lincoln County War** (Ed.) by Robert N. Mullin (University of Arizona Press, Tucson, 1968).

5. It was a double ceremony, the other couple being Barney Mason and Juana Madril. For a biographical sketch of Mason, who aided in the hunt for Billy the Kid, see "Garrett's Favorite Deputy" by Philip J. Rasch (Potomac Westerner's **Corral Dust**, Volume IX, Number 4, Fall, 1964), pp. 3-5.

6. Billy the Kid, born Henry McCarty, and sometimes known by his stepfather's name of Antrim, has been the subject of a vast amount of written material, far in excess of his actual historical or criminal importance. The

greater part of it has been generally inaccurate and hardly worthy of serious attention, but in the past decade or so a small band of dedicated researchers, working together or independently, have managed to separate much of the fact from the fiction or hearsay, particularly regarding his early life. See "New Light on the Legend of Billy the Kid" by Philip J. Rasch and Robert N. Mullin (**New Mexico Historical Review**, Volume VIII 1953-54), pp. 6-11; "Billy the Kid: The Real Story" by Philip J. Rasch and Robert N. Mullin (English Westerners' **Brand Book**, July, 1956), pp. 2-7; "A Man Named Antrim" by Philip J. Rasch (Los Angeles Westerners' **Brand Book**, Volume 6, 1956), pp. 48-54; "More on the McCartys" by Philip J. Rasch (English Westerners' **Brand Book**, April, 1957), pp. 3-9; "Clues to the Puzzle of Billy the Kid" by Philip J. Rasch (English Westerners' **Brand Book**, December, 1957 — January, 1958), pp. 8-11; "And One Word More" by Philip J. Rasch (**New Mexico Historical Review**, Volume XXXVI, 1961), pp. 41-42; "The Bonney Brothers" by Philip J. Rasch (**Frontier Times**, Austin, Volume 39, Number 1, New Series Number 33, December, 1964 — January, 1965), p. 43 et seq; also "Billy the Kid: The Trail of a Kansas Legend" by Waldo E. Koop (Kansas City Westerners' **Trail Guide**, Volume IX, Number 3, September, 1964); and **The Boyhood of Billy the Kid** by Robert N. Mullin ("Southwestern Studies," Volume V, Number 1, Texas Western Press, El Paso, 1967).

7. For a biographical sketch of O'Folliard, see "The Short Life of Tom O'Folliard" by Philip J. Rasch (Potomac Westerners' **Corral Dust**, Volume VI, May, 1961), p. 9 et seq.

8. For an inadequate biography — but the only one of this man, see **Dave Rudabaugh — Border Ruffian** by F. Stanley (World Press, Denver, 1961).

9. For a sketch of Wilson, see "Amende Honorable — The Life and Death of Billy Wilson" by Philip J. Rasch (**West Texas Historical Association Yearbook**, Volume XXXIV, October, 1958), pp. 97-111.

10. For a biographical sketch of Pickett, see "He Rode With the Kid: The Life of Tom Pickett" by Philip J.Rasch (English Westerners' **Tenth Anniversary Publications**, 1964), pp. 11-15.

11. Charlie Bowdre appears to have been trying to get out of the rustling business. On 15th December, 1880, he wrote to Captain J.C. Lea of Roswell to this effect, and gave grounds for thinking that he might be prepared to turn in the Kid, if his own immunity from prosecution was guaranteed. The original letter is in the Hungtington Library, San Marino, California, and a facsimile is reproduced in **Little Known Facts About Billy the Kid** by Peter Hertzog (Press of the Territorian, Santa Fe, 1963), pp. 12-14.

12. John W. Poe was born in Mason County, Kentucky, on 17th October, 1850, and, like Garrett, became a buffalo hunter in Texas. He was Town Marshal of Fort Griffin for a year and in 1879, while living at Fort Elliot, ran for office as Sheriff of Wheeler County. He lost to Henry Fleming by only one vote. He was a Deputy United States Marshal prior to moving to New Mexico where he became a deputy under Garrett and then succeeded him as Sheriff of Lincoln County. He died at Roswell, New Mexico, on 17th

July, 1923 — of pneumonia, it was stated officially; by his own hand, said others.

13. Garrett's account of the killing of the Kid appeared in his book (University of Oklahoma Press edition), pp. 142-49, and John W. Poe also set down a version which appeared in the English magazine **Wide World** in December, 1919. It was subsequently published in the United States (Houghton Mifflin, Boston, 1933) and more recently as **The True Story of the Killing of Billy the Kid** by John W. Poe, as told to E.A. Brininstool, (Frontier Press, Houston, 1958).

14. Jarvis P. Garrett, op. cit., p. 21.

15. The concept of the book caused mixed emotions in New Mexico. The Mora **Pioneer** hailed it and commented: "Every citizen should purchase at least ten copies of the work to assist the writer" — Mora **Pioneer,** reprinted in Las Vegas **Gazette,** 22nd October, 1881. The **Gazette,** however, did not approve and remarked: "Mr. Garrett, as Sheriff, took the life of a noted desperado, and the people have rewarded him. This would have satisfied some men. We see no pressing necessity for the work he is to have printed, and can only look on it as a means of reaping a further harvest from a lucky shot" — Ibid. On 30th November, 1881, Garrett signed a contract with the New Mexico Printing and Publishing Company to produce a book on the life and times of Billy the Kid. It was not a good contract, his son said later, for not only was the company lacking in "sufficient competence in the field of marketing to achieve even average success, but "the percentage [to Garrett] stipulated under the contract was very small" — Jarvis P. Garrett, op. cit., p. 7. J.C. Dykes, op. cit., p. xviii, gives some interesting details concerning the writing and printing history of **The Authentic Life.** Both Jarvis P. Garrett and J.C. Dykes deal with Pat Garrett's co-author, an itinerant Connecticut newspaperman and friend of the family named Marshall Ashmun Upson, known as Ash Upson — Dykes, pp. xvi-xvii, and Jarvis P. Garett, pp. 22-24.

16. Pat Garrett's commission was dated 10th March, 1884, and a good account of his activities as Captain of Texas Rangers is to be found in **Maverick Town: The Story of Old Tascosa** by John L. McCarty (University of Oklahoma Press, Norman, 1946), pp. 129-39.

17. Jarvis P. Garrett, op. cit., p. 21.

18. Garrett moved to Uvalde on 20th October, 1889, and his family followed in the spring of 1891. The final sale of his Roswell property was not completed until the early part of 1892, Ash Upson remaining on the ranch to conclude the deal for Garrett and joining the family at Uvalde when the negotiations were completed — Jarvis P. Garrett, op. cit., pp. 22-34. His son also comments on Pat Garrett's gambling and the family's financial problems.

19. Ibid., pp. 24-26, quoting from family letters sent from Las Cruces by Garrett to his wife on 25th February and 1st, 8th, 12th and 22nd March, 1896. In the last letter he said that the office of Sheriff had been turned over to him and that the reward money had been increased to $12,000.

20. Oliver Milton Lee was born at Buffalo Gap, Texas, on 8th November, 1865, and first trailed a horse herd into New Mexico in the fall of 1884 with his half-brother Perry Altman. He remained in New Mexico for the rest of his life, a long, violent, sometimes selfish, but ultimately useful one. His marriage to Winnie P. Rhode made him brother-in-law to W.W. Cox.

21. William McNew was one of the pioneer ranchers of the Tularosa region and had a ranch on the edge of the White Sands at a place known as "Point of Sands."

22. The principal work on Fountain is **The Life and Death of Colonel Albert Jennings Fountain** by A.M. Gibson (University of Oklahoma Press, Norman, 1965). This book seeks to pin the killing of Fountain and his son upon Oliver Lee, and the author is often seemingly reluctant to present documentary evidence which would weaken his case against Lee. Considerable material concerning Fountain's early life — especially his adventures in Nicaragua with the filibuster William Walker — is left out, and though Gibson seeks to imply the hand of Lee in Pat Garrett's death in 1908 no evidence is presented or even discussed. In short the book is unsatisfactory, although it does fill a gap in Southwestern biography, at least until a better work on Fountain comes along. There are certainly good points in the book — like the assessment of the corrupt "Santa Fe Ring" and the exhaustive use of the reports of Pinkerton Operative J.C. Fraser. However, the villains could hardly be more villainous or the hero more heroic. None of the men were all bad and Fountain himself was a far from easy man, one who might be expected to get into trouble. The other major works dealing with the death of Fountain and Pat Garrett's hunt for his killers are Sonnichsen, **Tularosa**, op. cit., especially pp. 123-90; and Keleher, **Fabulous Frontier**, op. cit., especially pp. 216-39. Hutchinson, **Another Verdict**, op. cit., was written in direct reply to Gibson's book.

23. James Robert Gililland, often known as "Jim-Bob," was born in Brown County, Texas, on 22nd March, 1874, and was taken to New Mexico at the age of twelve. A rough, sometimes violent, man who carved an empire for himself, "Jim-Bob" is remembered with affection in the range country. He lived a long and full life which ended at Hot Springs, Sierra County, New Mexico, on 8th August, 1946.

24. The warrants were issued by Judge Frank W. Parker on 2nd April, 1898.

25. According to Jarvis P. Garrett, op. cit., p. 31, Albert Bacon Fall's weekly newspaper **The Independent Democrat** was used as a pro-Lee mouthpiece to propagate this view and "if Lee had had the opportunity he could have killed Garrett and would have automatically had a perfect alibi for murder in self defence." He said, p. 33, that Lee put it about that he would "not surrender to Pat Garrett because he feared that his life was in jeopardy." Keleher, **Fabulous Frontier**, op. cit., p. 222, bears this out and cites letters Lee wrote to Fall's newspaper.

26. "Black Jack" Christian operated extensively in Oklahoma during 1895 and the early part of 1896 and then shifted his activities to New Mexico and Arizona. His gang was called "The High Five" and after nine months of

banditry — at the end of which Christian was shot — they virtually disbanded. Les Dow played an active part in helping to smash the gang — see **'Black Jack' Christian: Outlaw** by Jeff Burton (Press of the Territorian, Santa Fe, 1967).

27. The Eddy **Current,** 17th October, 1895, reported Les Dow's arrest of Bill McNew, and added: "Dow says there has been a wholesale theft of cattle by a certain gang in Lincoln County, among the principal leaders of the gang being McNue (sic) and Oliver Lee." Ibid., 13th February, 1896, reports that Dow had left for El Paso to help in the investigation of Fountain's murder. Some details concerning this are contained in "Biographical Sketch of Les Dow" by his son Hiram M. Dow, manuscript in the University of Oklahoma Library. Les Dow, properly James L. Dow, was born in Clinton, De Witt County, Texas, on 30th April, 1860, and was one of the best-known lawmen in West Texas and New Mexico. He had been a Cattle Inspector for the Texas and New Mexico Sanitary Association and a detective for the New Mexico Livestock Association, performing sterling service in both positions. He took over as Sheriff of Eddy County, New Mexico, in January, 1897, and was killed on 18th February. Dave Kemp was tried for the murder but was acquitted. Additional material on Les Dow is contained in a series of letters from Hiram M. Dow, of Mayhill, New Mexico, to CR, 24th July, 16th, 18th, and 28th August, and 16th September, 1966. Gibson, **Fountain,** op. cit., p. 262, hints that Dow's death may well have been closely connected with the Fountain case, and Keleher, **Fabulous Frontier,** op. cit., (1962 edition), p. 240 suggests that Dow "might have lived to the proverbial ripe old age if he had not been a witness before the Lincoln County grand jury which handed up indictments against several prominent men at the instigation of special prosecutor Fountain." For an account of Dow's hunt for the "Black Jack" Christian gang see Rickards, **Ballard,** op. cit., pp. 13-15, and Burton, **Christian,** op. cit., pp. 20-22.

28. Accounts of the Wildey Well fight are to be found in Keleher, **Fabulous Frontier,** op. cit., p. 220-23; Sonnichsen, **Tularosa,** op. cit., p. 159-64; Gibson, **Fountain,** op. cit., pp. 266-67; **A Bar Cross Man: The Life and Personal Writings of Eugene Manlove Rhodes** by W.H. Hutchinson (University of Oklahoma Press, Norman, 1956), p. 62; and Jarvis P. Garrett, op. cit., pp. 32-33.

29. Albert Bacon Fall's shadow loomed over early New Mexico Territory. In time he became a nationally known politician of great ability. He was born in Frankfort, Kentucky, on November 21, 1861, and arrived in New Mexico at the age of 20. He was the Territory's most prominent and controversial lawyer and was involved in one capacity or another in virtually every major legal case until 1911 when he entered the political arena with his customary dash and flair — see David H. Stratton (Ed.), "The Memoirs of Albert B. Fall," ("Southwestern Studies," Volume IV, Number 3, Texas Western Press, El Paso, 1966); also "New Mexican Machiavellian? — The Story of Albert B. Fall" by David H. Stratton (**Montana, The Magazine of Western History,** Helena, Autumn, 1957); "For The Defense — Albert Bacon Fall" by George Topping (Chicago Westerners' **Brand Book,** Volume XII,

Number 9, November, 1955), contains a sketch of him, as does Keleher, **Fabulous Frontier,** op. cit., pp. 180-201.

30. Thomas Benton Catron (1840-1921) was a colorful and extremely controversial figure in Territorial New Mexico. A most useful sketch of his life is to be found in Keleher, **Fabulous Frontier,** op. cit., pp. 97-118.

31. A quite excellent analytical article on the whole Fountain business, drawn from the published studies, interviews, primary source materials and contemporary newspapers, is "Death in Dona Ana County," Part 1, by William R. Smith (English Westerners' **Brand Book,** Volume 9, Number 2, January, 1967, Publication Number 125), pp. 1-11. This is an intelligent and well-thought-out article, meticulously documented.

32. Mullin, "Two Forgotten Killings," art. cit., pp. 59-62; Phil Cooke, Santa Fe, to CR, 14th February, 1969. It was widely mouthed about that Garrett and not Espalin had fired the fatal shot.

33. Theodore Roosevelt was born in New York City on 27th October, 1858. He did not enjoy reading law, and in early life showed an inclination towards history and natural history. He ranched in the Dakota Badlands for a time and entered politics in 1882. He was Assistant Secretary of the Navy in President William McKinley's administration, but resigned on 6th May, 1898, to help Leonard Wood raise the "Rough Riders." He was the hero of San Juan Hill, and when Wood was promoted became Colonel of the "Rough Riders" Regiment. After the war he became Vice-President under McKinley and upon the President's assassination he assumed his office, taking the oath on 14th September, 1901. His list of literary works is long and the quality of them extremely varied. One of his books told of his old Regiment, **The Rough Riders** (1899). He died 6th January, 1919.

34. Garrett's appointment, though announced mid-way through the month, did not become effective until 20th December, 1901. Keleher, **Fabulous Frontier,** op. cit., p. 72 mentions the protests. Sonnichsen, **Tularosa,** op. cit., p. 236, says that most of them came from Republicans who wanted the office for themselves.

35. Jarvis P. Garrett, op. cit., pp. 38-39, quoting letter from Pat Garrett to President Roosevelt, dated 8th February, 1903.

36. Ibid., pp. 37-38, quoting letter from John Nance Garner, Uvalde, Texas, 14th December, 1901, to Pat Garrett.

37. Ibid.

38. George Curry had been a young boy in the heyday of Dodge City, Kansas, and arrived in New Mexico in the late 1870s. He knew all the old-time lawmen and outlaws and counted many of them as his friends. From his position as Manager of the Block Ranch in Lincoln County — owned by Dowlin and Delaney of Fort Stanton — he progressed in many directions. He was Sheriff of Lincoln County, 1892-94, and in 1898 became a Captain of "Rough Riders" and a personal friend of Theodore Roosevelt, but did not get to Cuba with the outfit. In 1899 he was Sheriff of the newly-created Otero County, but resigned to accept a commission in the Eleventh Volunteer Regiment and was sent to the Philippines where, after military

service, he was appointed chief of Police in Manila and later a civil governor. For his life story see **George Curry, 1861-1947, An Autobiography,** (Ed.) by H.B. Henning, from Curry's manuscript materials (University of New Mexico Press, Albuquerque, 1958). His version of, and observations regarding, the Fountain murder occupy pp. 100-19.

39. Jarvis P. Garrett, op. cit., p. 40-41, referring to W.B. Childers, Attorney, Albuquerque, to Pat Garrett, 6th June, 1906.

40. **Life of Pat Garrett and the Taming of the Border Outlaw** by John Milton Scanland (Carleton F. Hodge, El Paso, 1908), p. 4. This exceedingly rare little booklet, written by a newspaperman who was a competent reporter and investigator, was published the year of Garrett's murder and contains much that is interesting concerning the events leading up to his death. The booklet is only 38 pages long, the first eleven of them given over to the last few months of his life and his murder. Scanland puts his finger on a number of crucial factors which materially influenced the last days of Pat Garrett and it is in this that the value of the work lies, for the material on his earlier days is patchy and inadequate. Much detail about Garrett's life is from Upson's book.

41. William H.H. Llewellyn was long prominent in public affairs, mostly political and promotional ones, in Nebraska and then in New Mexico. He was one of the men involved in naming Oliver Lee, Jim Gililland and William McNew as the killers of Colonel Albert Fountain and his son, and, like Curry, was a Captain in the "Rough Riders."

42. Pat Garrett to Major W.H.H. Llewellyn, from Las Cruces, dated 21st June, 1907 — cited in Jarvis P. Garrett, op. cit., p. 49. It is suggested by Garrett's son that the $2,000 was needed as an outright "cancellation of the debt," with no strings attached — Ibid., p. 41.

43. Scanland, op. cit., p. 4. Bill Isaacs, of Las Cruces, said in an interview on 15th September, 1954, that Garrett had not paid his taxes and borrowed $3,500 from Cox, but he did not mention the $2,000 owing to the merchant — Sonnichsen, **Tularosa,** op. cit., p. 318. It is believed that this sum was intended to clear both the taxes and the debt. Jim Cox, son of W.W. Cox, believes that his father lent Garrett a total of $5,500.

44. In 1953 author Eugene Cunningham, cowboy and seafarer, who had known most of the more colorful men in El Paso in the decade before the First World War, wrote to historian W.H. Hutchinson of Chico, California, and gave his assessment of Pat Garrett's behavior during the last few years of his life. Cunningham's informants were such men as W.W. Cox, Oliver Lee, Albert B. Fall, all of them Garrett's enemies, but he was able to assess their undoubtedly prejudiced views against those of men who had been Garrett's friends and the comments of others who had not taken sides and who, therefore, were in the position of the traditional bystander who sees all, or almost all. Maury Kemp told Cunningham that liquor made Garrett even more dangerous and swift and said that many were deadly afraid of him and of his often bullying ways. Robert N. Mullin, noted historian of the Southwest, had the advantage of many in having grown up in turn-of-the-

century El Paso. His father knew Garrett, who on at least one occasion was a guest at the Mullin home. Mr. Mullin remembers that Garrett was a boyhood hero to the El Paso youngsters and there was delight among the young Mullins when the demi-god arrived. "Garrett repulsed our friendly overtures when we boys tried to talk with him," Mr. Mullin recalls. "He was morose and surly." The views of both Cunningham and Mullin were expressed in letters to Hutchinson and are quoted in **Another Verdict,** op. cit., pp. 15 and 10 respectively. Sonnichsen, **Tularosa,** op. cit., p. 229, notes that the El Paso **Daily Herald** of 29th February, 1908, carried a story that Garrett had received an anonymous death threat in the form of a letter. Keleher, **Fabulous Frontier,** op. cit., p. 72, reports that Garrett pistol-whipped Jim Baird, though men who knew Baird say the story is untrue and Baird would have killed Garrett if he had tried such a play.

45. It has been suggested — Sonnichsen, **Tularosa,** op. cit., p. 257, quoting an interview with Maury Kemp, on 13th August, 1954, and Keleher, **Fabulous Frontier,** op. cit., (1962 edition) p. 87, quoting a letter from Kemp in 1945 — that Roosevelt was annoyed that Garrett took Tom Powers to the "Rough Riders" Convention, but Garrett's son denies this, and also the story that his father's re-appointment as Collector of Customs was refused because of the President's anger. These allegations, he says, are "without founda- tion" — Jarvis P. Garrett, op. cit., p. 40. Others in a position to know uphold Kemp's story and say that Roosevelt was furious over the incident. The description of the "Coney Island" was given in the El Paso **Times,** 14th May, 1909.

46. Jarvis Garrett, op. cit., p. 41.

CHAPTER 2
A MURDER IS PLANNED

In the late summer of 1907 the enemies of Pat Garrett set in motion a train of events which would lead in less than six months to his death. In the beginning, however, they may have hoped that it would not come to that, may have felt that he could possibly be squeezed out of the San Andres country through pressure.

There were various reasons why Garrett's continued presence in the area was a source of annoyance to some. Vengeance was undoubtedly one of them, and the fear that he might take up the Fountain murder case again and unearth new evidence, but a very strong factor was that Pat Garrett controlled water on his range, and water was something which could make a cattleman if he had it and break him if he did not.

Over the years there had been several killings over range rights and water in the region and Oliver Lee, whether he had a hand in the Fountain murders or not, had shed rather more than his share of blood to defend his own interests and build himself an empire. Eugene Manlove Rhodes,[1] ex-cowboy and noted author whose pictures of range life, especially New Mexico range life, caught the old-time flavor better than most, was a close friend of Lee's. He never believed him guilty of the Fountain killings, but knew of others who had gone down before Lee's gun. Shortly before he died Rhodes said: "Oliver Lee has killed eight men."[2] Author Eugene Cunningham,[3] nearly as knowledgeable as Rhodes about the life and ways of the New Mexican warriors of yesteryear, thought it more than probable, even considered that the figure might have been rather higher.[4] Walter Good was one of Lee's victims[5] and so later were Charlie Rhodius and Matt Coffelt. Albert B. Fall turned up to represent Lee in court, claiming that the two men had stolen his cattle and then resisted him when he tried to recover his property. Others who were around at the time said that the killings were wanton murder.[6] An old Frenchman who had a piece of land not far away from Lee's Dog Canyon Ranch was visited by three men one Christmas Eve and left lying dead in the doorway of his stone hut. His assassins were never indicted and nobody filed for his water rights for several years but when they were claimed it was Oliver Lee who signed the papers.[7]

Jarvis P. Garrett said later that his father was considered to be an "intruder," by his neighbors, including W.W. Cox, the nearest of them, and added: "He had good range land and what's more, spring water for which the ranchers thirsted."[8] An old range man who did business with

Cox at the turn of the century and assessed the situation with the instinct and feel of what makes trouble in cattle country, said: "Garrett had got a bit of water in the heart of the Cox range and moved in a bunch of stock horses. This I think was the impelling motive."[9]

Cox, of course, also harbored deep feelings against Garrett dating back to the 1899 killing of the man Reed, which had brought about a miscarriage on the part of Mrs. Cox.

Salty W.W. Cox was as tough as the next man, maybe tougher, and had never hesitated to take up a gun to defend what he considered to be his honor, his rights, his family or his own personal interests. He had seen his share of blood and violence during the Sutton-Taylor feud, which rocked a goodly portion of Texas in the two decades following the Civil War, and knew how to look after himself. The feud had started in DeWitt County, cattle-raising country between San Antonio and the Gulf Coast, and initially involved only the Taylor and Sutton families and their most immediate relatives. However, as the guns barked, and the mounting deaths on either side began to thin the family ranks, others were dragged in, some of them distant kith and kin, others with connections of friendship rather than blood or marriage. The Texas Rangers were on the scene now and again when the feud became too notorious or bloody. Some of the participants went to jail while others left the county, usually pursued by both bullets and posses.

Bill Cox sided with the Suttons and was present in the little town of Clinton on 27th December, 1875, when Jim Taylor rode in with his friends. The Taylor sympathizers said later that they came to surrender. The Suttons' story had it that they intended to burn down the courthouse and destroy incriminating paperwork, including a whole sheaf of varied indictments. Either way, the factions clashed and when the smoke cleared away Jim Taylor and two of his men were found lying riddled against a fence which they had not succeeded in climbing in their wild attempt to escape. Young Jim's death left the Taylors leaderless and the feud suddenly altered shape, became less an affair between families and friends and taking on new alliances fighting over new grievances.

Taylors had ambushed old Captain Jim Cox, patriarch of the family, back in 1873 and the clan were less than likely to forget it. In the summer of 1876 Bill Cox got into a scrap with George Brassell, who was said to have been involved in the bushwhacking of Captain Jim, and although no blood was drawn feelings ran high. On a moonless night, 19th September, somebody put an end to George Brassell, and his doctor father. It led to court action with Bill Cox, his brother-in-law Jack Ryan, Dave Augustine, Joe Sitterlie, William Meador and Jim Hester finding themselves on murder charges. Texas Rangers were called in and collected the six men at a wedding dance being held to celebrate the marriage of Melissa Cox to Joe Sitterlie. They took Frank Heidrichs along too. A few days later the men were joined in jail by Charles Heisig, indicted on the same charges.

When the cases came to trial in December, 1877, Heisig had an independent hearing and was turned loose. Dave Augustine and Jim Hester came clear of the charge of killing George Brassell, but were remanded to jail again for the murder of the old doctor. William Meador's case ended in a hung jury and for the next seventeen years his name appeared on various court dockets in nearby counties and was not finally dismissed until 1894. Bill Cox and his brothers-in-law Jack Ryan and Joe Sitterlie were convicted of murder in the first degree in a San Antonio court in April, 1878, and though they lost their subsequent appeal some key paperwork mysteriously disappeared and a new hearing had to be ordered. A trial in March, 1880, led to a judgement against the men for murder in the second degree, but a fatal flaw in the wording of the indictment was ruled to invalidate the proceedings and called for a reversal and further remand. Bail was granted.

Cox deemed it prudent to remove himself from Texas during this lull and went to the Organ Mountains country of New Mexico, where he was soon joined by his two brothers-in-law. On the last day of 1891 the three, men, plus Dave Augustine, were re-indicted. Only Augustine faced a court at the time. Some eighteen months later he pleaded that he had already been acquitted of the murder of Dr. Brassell and wangled a change of venue. In 1896 he got a further charge, but was convicted and given twenty-five years for the crime. He appealed and lost, but the Governor, taking into account Augustine's military record with a Confederate regiment, issued a pardon in October, 1899, over twenty-three years after the murder had been committed. Jack Ryan went back to Texas to face the music and was bailed in August, 1894, and again in January, 1896. Jim Hester also obtained bail in November, 1895. The two cases do not appear to have gone further.[10]

W.W. Cox had settled in New Mexico and had no intention of involving himself in costly and lengthy litigation which might or might not end in his freedom. He stayed where he was and kept the peace. Nobody ever came for him with a warrant or extradition order from Texas. He took no chances, however, and it was known among his close associates that he never went further into Texas than El Paso, just in case.[11]

The first step in planning the harassment of Pat Garrett was taken in the early fall of 1907, when a meeting was called at the St. Regis Hotel in El Paso. At least six men were present, possibly more. The meeting was convened by W.W. Cox[12] and his brother-in-law Oliver Lee was almost certainly among those present. Jim Gililland was also probably there, but not William McNew, the third of the men who had been charged by Garrett with the Fountain killing. Those in a position to know have said that Lee and McNew had fallen out and were not on speaking terms.[13] Lee's lawyer Albert B. Fall attended the meeting and played a key part in putting into effect the plans which were made at it. A saloon-keeper named A.P. Rhode, brother-in-law of Cox and known to his friends as "Print," was also there. Like Cox, he had been a pro-Lee and Gililland witness in the Fountain murder trial. The most important person present, however, was James P. Miller, a notorious figure in the history of West Texas and Southeastern New Mexico, as well as farther afield, known and feared as a gun for hire and called "Killer" Miller by some, and "Killing Jim" by others. He was accompanied by two of his relatives-by-marriage, Carl Adamson of Roswell — a general ne-er-do-well and petty criminal — and Mannie Clements — gambler, sometime peace officer and son of Emanuel — Manning — Clements, the well-known old-time Texas cattleman.

The men who gathered at the St. Regis Hotel agreed that the first step should be to put pressure on Pat Garrett in an effort to force him out of the country. Failing that, it was decided, he would have to be killed. It was to discuss how this second step should be handled, if the need came, that Jim Miller and his relatives had been brought in. Miller's fee for killing Garrett has been argued about over the years, the most popular figures of $1,500, $5,000 and $10,000 being quoted. It would seem that $5,000 is most probably correct, for Miller had earned more than $1,500 for killing men not half so well-known as Garrett. One of his stipulations was that W.W. Cox must find somebody who would take the blame for the murder, and also that a witness be furnished to support a claim of self-defense. After some discussion it was agreed that the murder fee would be handed to Mannie Clements, who would collect it from Albert Fall's office if and when it became necessary to kill Garrett. Cox undertook to find someone who would take the blame for the murder and keep his mouth shut. He had such a man in mind, one of his cowboys named Wayne Brazel. Carl Adamson was to be the witness, probably on Miller's insistence, as he would have wanted somebody upon whom he could rely implicitly. It was further agreed that Fall would do his best to curb the enthusiasm of those who would undertake the investigation which must inevitably follow Garrett's murder, and that he would not only defend Wayne Brazel, but would also use his influence to ensure that the hearing was held in a "friendly" court. A "pot" was taken up to cover the expenses of the whole exercise — including Miller's fee if it was decided later that Garrett must die — and the meeting adjourned.[14]

The first step in the conspiracy was comparatively simple.

W.W. Cox held a mortgage on most of Garrett's land and some of his cattle in exchange for the $3,500 which had been borrowed by Garrett to pay off his previous mortgage to the Las Cruces merchant and to pay his back taxes. George Curry had still not paid Garrett all the money he owed him, and the time for the redemption of the mortgage to Cox was running out. Additionally, Garrett had borrowed from a bank to buy the blooded stock he needed for the breeding and raising of quarter horses at his San Andres ranch. Cox had learned that Garrett was trying to raise another loan in the northern part of the Territory and was offering a first mortgage as security. He was not sure whether this was on the land that Garrett had already mortgaged to him, on his Bear Canyon ranch, his home ranch or even on cattle and other stock, and he cautioned his foreman to keep a close watch on the animals running in Cox pastures. [15] It had been agreed that Cox would simply allow the mortgage to lapse, which he did, and the bank, frightened that their money was not safe, obtained a writ of attachment on the stock Garrett was running under his own brand. [16] Cox had been holding some of Garrett's cattle on his own ranges — to assist Garrett in keeping it clear of creditors — and most of the cows had been given the Cox brand. [17] Cox simply attached the stock — to prevent the bank from getting them — and then conveyed them back to Garrett. However, now Garrett had insufficient stock to run on his property at Bear Canyon. [18] Cox then offered to buy Garrett out, offering a good price in the hope that he would take it and move away altogether.

It was Garrett's last chance to get some money and to save his life, but he could not know it. Hoping that something would turn up and enable him to keep his home, he turned Cox's offer down flat. [19]

Up at his ranch Cox knew that it would now be necessary to kill Garrett and the others in the conspiracy were so informed. The plan was a complex and careful one, calling for the involvement of at least eight people, and Cox set wheels in motion. On his suggestion Wayne Brazel, one of the cowboys at Cox's San Augustine ranch, approached Garrett with a proposition to lease the grazing rights of the Bear Canyon ranch. The idea suited Garrett and he concluded a deal with Brazel. He was made to understand that "Print" Rhode was Brazel's partner [20] and saw nothing odd in the fact that an ambitious young man wanted grazing land for a few calves as the first step to building up a herd of his own.

Garrett had stopped drinking and was more his former self at this time. He had been thinking about the Fountain case — and, no doubt, the reward money — and had privately re-opened the investigation. His son Jarvis was later to refer to his father's "tenaciousness" in hunting for the murderers and added that there was always a chance of "his unearthing new evidence."[21] It is possible that Garrett was making some progress at the time he was killed. Those who pretended to know said that this was the reason for his death. It may well have been a contributory factor, may even have accelerated the plans, but by the winter of 1907-08 Pat Garrett had too many enemies, who had too many reasons to allow him to live.

Word was sent to "Killing Jim" Miller at his home in Fort Worth, Texas.

NOTES
CHAPTER 2

1. Eugene Manlove Rhodes was born in Nebraska on 19th January, 1869, and spent his young manhood in New Mexico. Much of his actual writing, both of books and short stories for **The Saturday Evening Post** and other leading magazines, was done either in the East or on the West Coast. His "feel" for the country, and the fact that instead of creating characters for his stories he often used real people, gave his works a special tone. Rhodes was passionately loyal to his friends at all times, whether they were up or down, popular or the subject of execration. Among his novels were **Bransford in Arcadia, Good Men and True, Stepsons of Light, Once in the Saddle** and two — **Copper Streak Trail** and **Desire of the Moth** — which owed something to the facts surrounding the Fountain case. A volume of short stories was called **West is West**, an essay entitled **Say Now Shibboleth**, and his two best-known works **The Rusty Knaves** and **Paso Por Aqui** considered classics. He died in California on 27th June, 1934. Hutchinson, **A Bar Cross Man**, op. cit., is an excellent "Life" of Rhodes making continuous and intelligent use of his personal correspondence, and an invaluable Checklist of Rhodes' writings in included, pp. 392-407. **The Hired Man on Horseback** by May D. Rhodes (Houghton Mifflin, Boston, 1938) is a biography written by his wife.

2. Hutchinson, **Another Verdict**, op. cit., p. 4, citing a letter from Eugene Manlove Rhodes.

3. Eugene Cunningham was born in Helena, Arkansas, in 1896 and grew up around Dallas and Fort Worth, Texas. He started writing during World War One and subsequently travelled extensively in Central America and sailed in the South Pacific. He wrote sea stories under a nom-de-plume. Among his many Western novels were **Diamond River Man, Train to Acapaz, Texas Sheriff, Red Range, Border Guns, Quick Triggers, Buckaroo, Riding Gun, Bravo Trail, Outlaw Justice** and a book which owed much to the circumstances of the Fountain affair called **Spiderweb Trail**. A short story entitled "Guns of His Father" (**All Western Magazine**, June, 1933) was based on the Garrett murder. **Triggernometry** (Caxton, Caldwell, Idaho, 1941; numerous reprintings, ninth, 1962, used here) was a collection of biographical sketches of old-time lawmen and outlaws. He died in San Francisco in 1957.

4. Hutchinson, **Another Verdict**, op. cit., p. 5, citing a letter from Eugene Cunningham.

5. Walter Good was killed in the White Sands on 20th August, 1888, and his father, John Good, was positive that Oliver Lee had been the killer — Keleher, **Fabulous Frontier**, op. cit., p. 214; Sonnichsen, **Tularosa**, op. cit., pp. 39-45; George Curry, **Autobiography**, op. cit., pp. 101-02.

6. Rhodius and Coffelt were killed by Lee and Jim Gililland on 12th February,

1893 — **Rio Grande Republican,** 17th February, 1893; Sonnichsen, **Tularosa,** op. cit., p. 87; The comment that it was wanton murder is quoted in Hutchinson, **Another Verdict,** op. cit., p. 7, his source being the "Cowman." George Curry, **Autobiography,** op. cit., p. 78 and p. 102, mis-spells the names of both men (Rhodis and Cofelt) and says that Bill McNew and Tom Tucker were present. A slightly garbled newspaper account of the killing, substantiating Curry's that Tucker at least was present, appeared in the St. Louis **Daily Globe-Democrat,** 14th February, 1893.

7. The Frenchman was Francois Jean Rochas and he was killed on 24th December, 1894 — Sonnichsen, **Tularosa,** op. cit., pp. 97-106. The matter of the water in Frenchy's Canyon caused trouble early in 1907. On 20th March, 1907, Lee and his men clashed at Winchester range with others who wanted the water at the old holding. No one was killed, but the incident was typical of water disputes in Southeastern New Mexico — El Paso **Times,** 20th and 23rd march, 1907; also Sonnichsen, **Tularosa,** op. cit., p. 197.

8. Jarvis P. Garrett, op. cit., p. 41. George Curry, **Autobiography,** op. cit., pp. 100-01, has some interesting comments to offer on range and water rights in the San Andres.

9. Hutchinson, **Another Verdict,** op. cit., p. 12, quoting his source the "Cowman." Garrett's land was not "in the heart of the Cox range" but at the extreme northwest corner.

10. William Webb Cox was born in DeWitt County, Texas, on 12th November, 1854, and it was in this county that the fiercest clashes of the Sutton-Taylor Feud occurred. The material on this protracted set of troubles is voluminous and scattered. The best overall picture of it is "Thirty Years A-Feuding" in **I'll Die Before I'll Run** by C.L. Sonnichsen (Devin-Adair, New York, 1962), pp. 35-115. Printed sources, newspapers, court records and interviews have been utilized by Dr. Sonnichsen in piecing together his story, and Bill Cox's involvement is dealt with in the closing section, notably pp. 90-115; Keleher, **Fabulous Frontier,** op. cit., (1962 edition), pp. 94-96, contains a biographical sketch of Cox. "San Augustine Ranch House" by Marshall Hail **(Frontier Times,** Austin, Volume 43, Number 5, New Series Number 61, August-September, 1969), pp. 38-40 et seq., contains an interesting — though occasionally inaccurate — article on Cox and the San Augustine Ranch, including some good pictures.

11. Hutchinson, **Another Verdict,** op. cit., quoting his source the "Cowman" who remarked: "One thing I know — you could not get Cox to go and set foot in Texas." This is not exactly true, as Cox did go to El Paso on business, but no further.

12. Ibid. The late Maurice Garland Fulton told W.H. Hutchinson that "a Mr. Hamlin, a retired lawyer who came out this way (Roswell), wormed it out of Curry that the person who hired the killer was W.W. Cox, Lee's brother-in-law. Many persons think that probable. Oliver stands acquitted" — pp. 9-10. Hutchinson's informant the "Cowman" also said that Cox was the leading figure in the negotiations — p. 12. The cowboy detective Charles A. Siringo

also points to Cox being a key man in the negotiations when he writes: "In about the year 1908, a few men who had smelled much powder smoke during and after the Civil War, in Texas, apparently raised ten thousand dollars to hire Jim Miller to kill Pat Garrett" — **Riata and Spurs** (Houghton Mifflin, Boston, 1931), p. 215. In "Death in Dona Ana County," Part 2, by William R. Smith (English Westerners' **Brand Book**, Volume 9, Number 3, April, 1967, Publication Number 128), pp. 1-5, is the statement: "Many people around Las Cruces believed that W.W. Cox was the man who so badly wanted Garrett out of the way" — p. 2. Smith cites as his authority a correspondent who wished to remain anonymous — "Private Correspondence from U.S.A." The "Hamlin" referred to by Maurice Garland Fulton was undoubtedly William Lee Hamlin, author of **The True Story of Billy the Kid** (Caxton, Caldwell, Idaho, 1959). Hamlin talked to a lot of old-timers in and around Lincoln County while collecting material for his book. The result, which contained some new material, and reproduced some documents not easily available, received a mixed reception from Lincoln County buffs. It was severly criticized by the American reviewer "Quago" (English Westerners' **Tally Sheet**, Volume VI, Number 2, January-February, 1960, Publication Number 54), pp. 19-21. He scoffed at the claim that twenty years of research went into the collecting of material, compared it with other works on Billy the Kid, and commented: "all things considered, it is one of the worst yet, not even excluding the fictional version of Walter Noble Burns." It is true that Hamlin is often careless with the spelling of names and confuses his story in places. He also seems not to be acquainted with recent scholarship in the publications of the various Westerners' groups, in **New Mexico Historical Review, West Texas Historical Association Yearbook, Panhandle-Plains Historical Review**, etc., and repeats some discredited stories about the Kid. However, it seems to this writer to have been an honest, if muddled, attempt to get at the truth. In **A Fitting Death for Billy the Kid** by Ramon F. Adams (University of Oklahoma Press, Norman 1960) the reception for Hamlin's book was the reverse of that of "Quago." Adams said it "appears to be the result of honest research and is above average in accuracy." Even so, he pointed out various shortcomings, and was "rather skeptical" about some of the conversations included by Hamlin, but concluded: "I think this book rather reliable, and it is encouraging to see the new trend of the Kid's biographers" — pp. 295-6. These comments brought "Quago" to the attack when reviewing Adams' book (English Westerners' **Tally Sheet**, Volume VI, Number 6, September-October, 1960, Publication Number 61), pp. 14-16. He testily commented that Adams' view of Hamlin's work must cause "the reader to wonder whether confidence can be placed in any of his judgements," and called the Adams book: "An interesting study of the developments of a legend at the hands of irresponsible writers and of its destruction by amateur historians, but one which is not up to the level of scholarship a reader has a right to expect from a university press, and which perpetuates parts of the legend it seeks to destroy."

13. Hutchinson, **Another Verdict**, op. cit., p. 7. His source the "Cowman" wrote: "Curry told me that Oliver Lee never spoke to McNew after the Fountain killings."

14. The facts of the meeting, the agreement to kill Garrett, the payment of the blood money to Mannie Clements in the office of an El Paso lawyer, the insistence of Miller that his "employers" find a man to confess to the murder as well as an eye-witness, were discovered by Fred Fornoff, Captain of the New Mexico Mounted Police, who made an investigation of the case in the late spring of 1908. Some of the information may have come from Mannie Clements himself — "The Assassination of Pat Garrett" by James Madison Hervey (**True West**, Austin, Volume 8, Number 4, Whole Number 44, March-April, 1961), p. 42. Hervey, a former Attorney-General of New Mexico, had been closely involved in the Garrett case. While collecting evidence in connection with the murder he kept notes of interviews, but after he was advised to leave well alone put them away. Some years later his secretary found them. Hervey commented that he must remember to burn them, and probably did so — Phil Cooke, Santa Fe, to CR, 28th February, 1968; see also "The Key to the Mystery of Pat Garrett" by Robert N. Mullin (Los Angeles Westerners' **Branding Iron**, No. 92, June, 1969), pp. 1, 4-5. Many years later Hervey set down his reminiscences, with the proviso that they were not to be published until eight years after his death, when he believed all those connected with the crime would be dead. The article was written in 1953. The fact that Cox convened the meeting is also known, though, as has been pointed out in Hutchinson, **Another Verdict**, op. cit., p. 18, "he was not alone in having a vested interest in Pat's taking-off. . . he was not the only contributor to the pot." Cautious Eugene Cunningham noted the meeting this way: "A group of well-to-do and known-to-each-other men MAYBE said one fine evening IF a funeral happened to Pat we'd all sleep sounder — Ibid., p. 16, citing a letter from Cunningham. Cox, Miller and Adamson were definitely at the meeting. The others named here are the ones my own investigation shows were also present.

15. "The Real Pat Garrett" by Bert Judia, as told to Eve Ball, (**Frontier Times**; Austin, Volume 38, Number 2, New Series Numer 28, February-March, 1964), p. 46.

16. Scanland, op. cit., p. 4.

17. Sonnichsen, **Tularosa**, op. cit., p. 229.

18. Scanland, op. cit., p. 4.

19. Sonnichsen, **Tularosa**, op. cit., p. 229.

20. Scanland, op. cit., p. 4; Siringo, **Riata and Spurs**, op.cit., p. 215, says that the duration of the lease was for five years.

21. Jarvis P. Garrett, op. cit., p. 36. James Madison Hervey, art. cit., p. 17, said: "Garrett continued the search. This he did long after his term as Sheriff had expired," and added, p. 46, that Garrett's death "grew out of his constant desire to find out who killed Fountain." Fountain's descendants apparently "still believe that Pat settled on his ranch in the San Andres because he thought the victims were buried on it or near it and he hoped to

continue the search unmolested" — Sonnichsen, **Tularosa,** op. cit., p. 194. Gibson, **Fountain,** op. cit., is extremely anti-Fall, Lee, Cox and their friends and allows tendentious phrases and one-sided presentation of the facts to case-make for him, so must be viewed with considerable care. It is his contention that "it was not secret that he [Garrett] had returned to southern New Mexico to complete a job he had begun in 1896. The fact that the Fountain reward money was still available no doubt was a strong inducement; added to this was Garrett's determination to vindicate himself — he still rankled at the public ridicule and shame which his failure to bring in the Fountain killers had stirred up," p. 287.

CHAPTER 3
JIM MILLER—GUN FOR HIRE

Jim Miller's name is writ large in the story of West Texas, Oklahoma and Southeastern New Mexico as an extinguisher of men. He killed for money, worked from ambush as a rule and considered a fast horse, a time-stamped telegram, and in the last eventuality a smart lawyer, to be the essential tools of his trade. He was not fussy about the type of firearm employed in his "business" transactions, using at various times pistol, rifle, or shotgun, and as well as handling killings on behalf of others, he was wont on occasion to take up weapons to pay off personal scores on his own account.

The very nature of Miller's "employment" precludes an accurate count of the men he put away, but he once boasted to Judge Charles R. Brice[1] that he had killed eleven men that people knew of, and hinted darkly that there had been others. The eleven killings, plus nine others whispered about, gave him a supremely dangerous reputation. Judge Brice called him "just a 'killer' — the worst man I ever knew."[2]

He was slim, 5 feet 10 inches tall, sported a handlebar moustache and dressed like a church deacon. Pleasant in manner, he made easy friends among the leading people in "respectable" quarters — who could never believe that he was as bad as he was made out — went to church regularly, never swore and neither smoked nor drank.[3] He served as a lawman at times, was in the hotel business for much of his adult life, conned a few people when he had the chance, paid off his scores with a permanency that defied retribution and would kill any man for money, his fees varying from $200 to $5,000 — depending upon the circumstances, the prominence of the victim and what he judged the market would stand. He was, first and foremost, a businessman.

Jim Miller was only eighteen years old when he shotgunned his brother-in-law John Coop to death at Plumb Creek, Coryell County, Texas, on the night of 30th July, 1884. The reason for the killing was never firmly established. Maybe they just did not get along. That would have been enough for Miller. He was tried and his alibi was broken, so the judge sentenced him to life imprisonment, but he won a retrial following a decision by the Texas Court of Appeals and came clear in due course, freed by his peers to embark upon a career as a hired killer second to none in the West.[4]

Only two years later he was running with a hard crowd in San Saba County, being especially friendly with the Renfro brothers,[5] who were noted stock-thieves in the area, and then turned up in Runnels County as an ally of the powerful Clements clan, headed by rugged old trail-driver Manning Clements. Miller's particular friend was young Mannie Clements Junior and he had a warm eye for pretty Sallie Clements. When old Manning clashed with Joe Townsend, City Marshal of Ball-inger, the family began muttering. The Clements brood had sided with the Taylors in the Sutton-Taylor feud which, though virtually over, still caused hatred and gunplay on occasions. John Wesley Hardin was blood kin, a very strong tie in that part of Texas at the time, and though he was in Hunstville Penitentiary there were plenty of other hard-cases about.

In due course the troubles between old Manning and Joe Townsend came to a head and on the night of 29th March, 1887, they met in the Senate Saloon in Ballinger. The City Marshal left the old trail driver dead on the floor. Jim Miller got into action before any of the family could avenge the patriarch's death. He ambushed Townsend by the trail one day, emptying a shotgun into him as he rode by. Doubtless the Clements clan were grateful for this show of togetherness, but they must have been disappointed with the result, for Townsend recovered, even though he did have to have an arm amputated.[6]

Miller later married Sallie Clements and shortly afterwards moved to Pecos, county seat of Reeves County, to join Mannie. The Millers opened an hotel. It was 1890 and Pecos was a wild frontier cattle town where people tended to their own business and expected others to do the same. Jim Miller joined a local church, attended regularly and was considered an asset to the community, being that his manners were so nice and he was a teetotal, non-smoking, non-swearing sort of fellow. Reeves County Sheriff G.A. "Bud" Frazer[7] made him a deputy. The two men worked well together and the good people of Pecos congratulated themselves on the high quality of their law enforcement officers.

The first blot on Miller's copybook was the killing of a Mexican prisoner he was taking to Fort Stockton.[8] The man had tried to escape, he explained. Soon afterwards, with stock-thefts increasing all the time, Frazer discovered that Miller was involved in a scheme to steal cattle in Texas and run them south into Mexico. Unfortunately for him Miller found out what Frazer had learned and formulated a plan to put him out of the way. In May, 1893, a small-time crook named J.C. "Con" Gibson tipped Frazer off that Miller, Mannie Clements and Mart. Q. Hardin[9] had asked him to help kill the Sheriff. Frazer at once swore out a complaint of "conspiracy to kill" against the three and Gibson was foolish enough to sign it.[10] Almost at once he told Frazer that the men had tried to tempt him into a cattle rustling operation and Frazer wired Texas Ranger John R. Hughes[11] to hurry to Pecos. Miller was arrested on 22nd July on a charge of mule-theft sworn out by Frazer[12] and the Rangers left. At once, prominent ranchers began urging Frazer to allow bail for his ex-deputy and eventually, with considerable reluctance, he agreed.[13] Day after day Miller sat on the porch of his hotel talking to his friends and biding his time for a showdown with Frazer. When the case was heard in El Paso it was thrown out for want of jurisdiction.[14]

"Con" Gibson heard about the dismissal and deemed it prudent to remove himself from Pecos prior to Miller's return. He took off to Eddy (now Carlsbad), New Mexico, but soon met John Denston, a cousin of Miller's wife. Denston was close to Miller, too, and considered it his bounden duty to do something abut Gibson. He did.[15] The news of Gibson's sudden demise reached Pecos about the time that the grand jury of Reeves County indicted Miller, Hardin and Clements on Frazer's "conspiracy to murder" complaint.[16] The actual hearing would not be held for several months and in the meantime Miller was loose, a fact which kept Frazer awake at nights.

The day after Christmas the Sheriff was abroad on the streets of Pecos and observed Jim Miller with his back to the street, talking to a friend. It seemed an ideal opportunity and Frazer opened fire. Miller was hit and his gun arm was disabled but he reached around behind him and got his pistol, at which point Frazer's nerve failed and he fled.[17] While recovering at a friend's home, Miller remarked: "I am going to kill Frazer if I have to crawl twenty miles on my knees to do it."[18] As soon as he was up and about he swore out a complaint charging Frazer with "assault with intent to murder."[19] Frazer did not intend to let it get to court for two reasons: at the very least it would nullify his own "conspiracy" complaint; and he had lost the election for another term as Sheriff and so no longer had the protection of a lawman's badge. On 12th April, 1894, he went after Miller with a Winchester. Miller had a shotgun, but the distance gave Frazer the advantage. He shot Miller in the arm and leg but the badman kept a-coming and when he got within shotgun range Frazer's nerve failed again and he turned and ran.[20] While Miller was recovering from his wounds Frazer left Pecos and went to live in Eddy where he opened a livery stable.

The "assault with intent" cases were scheduled for November, 1895, and Miller engaged John Wesley Hardin, freshly released from Huntsville Penitentiary and newly-qualified as a lawyer, to represent him. The cases were granted a change of venue at the request of Frazer's lawyers, but Wes Hardin did not appear in court.[21] He was three months dead, a casualty of bad company and a bullet in the back of the head in tough El Paso.[22] "Bud" Frazer was acquitted at Colorado City in May, 1896, mainly because of Jim Miller's own unsavory record.[23]

It was hardly to be expected that it would be the end of the affair and

Frazer returned to Eddy and watched his back. He was less careful when traveling, however, and it soon came to Jim Miller's attention that Fraser liked to visit a particular saloon in Toyah, a village some twenty-odd miles from Pecos. On 13th September, 1896, with the connivance of his friend, John Earhart, he went to Johnson's Saloon in Toyah where Frazer was playing cards, pushed open the door with a double-barreled shotgun and blew off his enemy's head. [24]

The trial came up in March, 1897, in Eastland and Jim Miller had taken the precaution of moving to the town, joining the church and getting to know the better citizens in the community. A goodly number of hard cases turned up for the event — Miller was claiming self-defense, of course, — and after a twenty-one day trial a hung jury of eleven for conviction and one against won him a new hearing. [25] The case was set for January, 1899, but a lot of blood would flow before that date. [26]

The late "Bud" Frazer's brother-in-law was a man named Barney Riggs, [27] a colorful and rugged individual who had killed his man and feared nobody. He decided that Miller needed cutting down to size, but before he could do anything about it he got into a scrape with Bill Earhart and John Denston. It was fatal for both of them [28] and though Riggs was acquitted [29] he felt it wise to give up any immediate ideas that he might have had about killing Miller. He had already served a jail term in Arizona Territory for murder, had killed a man while in prison and with the deaths of Denston and Earhart on his hands it might have appeared to some that killing was becoming a habit. He went back to Fort Stockton. [30]

A man called Joe Earp [31] had attended Miller's trial in Eastland and after the court ordered a new trial the two men got together and hatched a plan. Earp was to testify in a case at Vernon that he had seen a man named Joe Beasley commit a murder in Collingsworth County. Beasley would be convicted and they would then split the reward money which had been offered for the capture and conviction of the killer. It was a neat plan, except for the fact that peace officer "Dee" Harkey [32] had been playing cards with Earp at the time he was supposed to have witnessed the murder. When Harkey heard what Earp's testimony was to be he warned the man that he could and would offer evidence to refute it. On the witness stand Earp got cold feet and changed his evidence, implicating Jim Miller as the instigator of the idea. [33]

Miller was arrested on a charge of attempting to procure perjury, Beasley was set free and Joe Earp left Vernon hurriedly to put some distance between himself and Jim Miller's vengeance.

District Attorney Stanley of the 46th Judicial District prosecuted Miller in the case and he was found guilty, but his lawyers appealed and the Court of Criminal Appeals reversed the decision of the trial judge.[34] Jim Miller headed for Fort Worth and happened to meet Judge Charles Brice on the train. He remarked that he intended to kill Joe Earp and told Brice to watch the newspapers. He knew that Brice could take no action against such a boast and enjoyed putting the jurist in an impossible position. They met again three weeks later, just after Joe Earp had been killed from ambush in Coryell County. "I rode a hundred miles that night to establish an alibi by sending a telegram," Miller remarked.[35] He had moved to Memphis by this time and was operating an hotel. When District Attorney Stanley arrived in town he stayed at a rival establishment, but that did not prevent Miller from having his revenge. The good D.A. died suddenly, unexpectedly and in pain. The doctor who examined him diagnosed arsenic poinsoning — but prudently wrote "peritonitis" on the death certificate.[36]

While living in Memphis, in some extraordinary manner, Miller became a Texas Ranger[37] and not long afterwards rode across into Collingsworth County with a man named Lawrence Angel. They killed a man there under very odd circumstances and were both arrested. Angel, however, took the murder on himself and was the only one indicted. People whispered that Jim Miller had done the killing for money, with an agreement with his "employer" that Angel take the blame. Judge Brice believed these to be the facts of the case.[38] Miller killed two men in Midland[39] then went north to Lawton, Oklahoma, to slay a third.[40] In 1902 he accepted a fee to murder a surveyor named Jim Jarrott[41] near Lubbock, Texas, and two years later shot Frank Fore in the lavatory of the Westbrook Hotel in Fort Worth.[42]

He was tried only for the Fore killing but got away with a plea of self-defense when two men, who were in the lobby at the time of the murder, swore they had been in the lavatory and that Fore drew first. Miller was operating an hotel in the town at the time and it became his headquarters. He liked Fort Worth and made it his home for what remained of his life. He left there briefly in the summer of 1906 for a trip to Oklahoma Territory to kill an Indian policeman for another of his "customers."

Jim Miller was nothing if not professional. He anticipated Al Capone's hired "torpedoes" by three decades and "Murder Incorporated" by half a century. When he accepted money to kill a man, that man would surely die. He made his plans with care, equipped himself with alibi in case the plans failed and then got on with the job.

When he received W.W. Cox's summons in early February, 1908, he packed his bag and left for El Paso.

NOTES
CHAPTER 3

1. Charles Rufus Brice was born 6th August, 1870, at Terrell, Texas, and went to school there before going on to study law in Memphis, Tennessee. He began his practice in Hall County, Texas, and was County Attorney 1896-1900. He later moved to Carlsbad, New Mexico, was a member of the Constitutional convention, served in the Legislature, 1909-10, and became a Judge of the Fifth Judicial District, 1918. He was a Supreme Court Judge from 1934 and Chief Justice, 1941-42 and 1947-50. Judge Brice retired on 21st December, 1950 and died on 12th October, 1963.

2. Judge Charles Brice, writing the Foreword to **Mean As Hell**, by D.R. "Dee" Harkey (University of New Mexico Press, Albuquerque, 1948; New American Library, New York, 1955), p. ix. This book has been severely criticized by many old-time New Mexicans, who, while they concede that Dee Harkey knew whereof he spoke in many cases, claim that he had an unfortunate tendency in his reminiscences to put himself in the central position of each adventure, even when he actually played only a minor part. Research among the files of frontier newspapers by this writer tends to confirm the verbal criticisms of Harkey's contemporaries.

3. Ibid., Brice, p. ix; Harkey, **Mean As Hell**, p. 113. Miller's middle initial varies in the official records, being given variously as B., P., or M.

4. Details of the case are reported in **James Miller vs State of Texas, 18,** Texas Court of Appeals, 232.

5. Harkey, **Mean As Hell**, op. cit., pp. 20-22.

6. **The Steer Branded Murder** by Judge Barry Scobee (Frontier Book Company, Toyahvale, 1952), p. 18.

7. G.A."Bud" Frazer was born in Fort Stockton, Texas, on 18th April, 1864, the son of a judge. As a young man he saw service in Baylor's Texas Ranger company and was based at Ysleta. On 31st December, 1887, he married Mattie Riggs of Fort Stockton. Her brother Barney, who subsequently featured in Jim Miller's activities, was in jail in Arizona for murder.

8. An account of the troubles between Jim Miller and Bud Frazer is to be found in the altogether excellent **Ten Texas Feuds** by C.L. Sonnichsen (University of New Mexico Press, Albuquerque, 1957), pp. 200-09. The chapter is entitled "A Gentleman from Pecos" and is drawn from court records, old-timers' reminiscences and contemporary newspapers.

9. Little is known of this man, but it is thought possible that he was some kind of kin to the notorious John Wesley Hardin. He was later on the side of the law, being Deputy United States Marshal at East Las Vegas, New Mexico, in mid-1895 — E.L. Hall, United States Marshal for New Mexico, to Attorney General, Washington, D.C., 24th August, 1895, Enclosure 12,300,

File No. 5,624, Department of the Attorney General, National Archives and Records Service, Washington, D.C.

10. Reeves County, Texas, Records, Case No. 150, **State of Texas vs M.Q. Hardin.**

11. John R. Hughes was born at Cambridge, Illinois, in 1855 and in his early youth went to Indian Territory to work. He joined the Texas Rangers on 10th August, 1887, and served with distinction, rising through the ranks to become Captain of D Company in 1893, and finally retiring on 31st January, 1915, having served for 28 years. **Border Boss** by Jack Martin (Naylor, San Antonio, 1942) contained his reminiscences as told to the author, and though undocumented appears to be substantially accurate. See also **Fighting Men of the West** by Dane Coolidge (E.P. Dutton, New York, 1932), Chapter Six, and Cunningham, **Triggernometry**, op. cit., Chapter Nine entitled "Bayard of the Chaparral." He died in 1947.

12. Martin, **Border Boss**, p. 151.

13. Sonnichsen, **Ten Texas Feuds**, op. cit., p. 201. Miller was released on bail following a visit to Frazer by rancher E.O. Lochausen, whose widow was interviewed by Dr. Sonnichsen.

14. El Paso **Times**, 17th July, 1910.

15. Ibid.

16. **State of Texas vs M.Q. Hardin,** op. cit.

17. Sonnichsen, **Ten Texas Feuds**, op. cit., p. 202.

18. Ibid., p. 203.

19. Reeves County, Texas, Records, Case No. 190, **State of Texas vs G.A. Frazer.**

20. El Paso **Times**, 13th April, 1894.

21. District Court Minutes, El Paso County, Texas, Volume 8, page 425, Cases No. 1789 and 1790, 39th District — Filed at El Paso City Council Building.

22. Hardin was killed on 19th August, 1895, while shaking dice in the Acme Saloon in El Paso — El Paso **Times**, 20th August, 1895. There is no adequate biography of Hardin, though he has been subjected to scrutiny by writers on numerous occasions. Most have used his own account **The Life of John Wesley Hardin, From the Original Manuscript, as Written by Himself** (Smith & Moore, Sequin, Texas, 1896; University of Oklahoma Press, Norman, 1961) as a basis for their own writings. A carefully annotated version of this book would fill a much-needed gap in Western criminology, but has not been forthcoming. Many dates given by Hardin — especially in the Kansas section — are at variance with those in contemporary newspapers, and a considerable amount of his Texas material is also open to correction. His career has been chronicled in **The Fastest Gun in Texas** by J.H. Plenn and C.H. La Roche (New American Library, New York, 1956); **They Died With Their Boots On** by Thomas Ripley (Doubleday, New York, 1935); and **Wes Hardin, Texas Gunman** by Lewis Nordyke (John Long, London, 1958) among others. Nordyke had the advantage of help from the Hardin family, but instead of producing a definitive account was content to write a second-rate work. Hardin appears in virtually every collection of stories about gunfighters — Cunningham, **Triggernometry**, op. cit., Chapter Two, entitled "Forty Notches," pp. 38-65, is perhaps the best of these short sketches —

and in every book on "Wild Bill" Hickok. An accurate partial account of his activities in Kansas is to be found in **They Called Him Wild Bill** by Joseph G. Rosa (University of Oklahoma Press, Norman, 1964), pp. 127-30. His life after being released from prison has been ill-recorded, with a version from Harkey, **Mean As Hell**, op. cit., pp. 63-74, and serious attempts to unscramble the truth in **Jeff Milton — A Good Man With A Gun** by J. Evetts Haley (University of Oklahoma Press, Norman, 1948), 226-251, and in **John Selman — Texas Gunfighter** by Leon Claire Metz (Hastings House, New York, 1966), pp. 159-81.

23. District Court Minutes, Mitchell County, Volume 1, page 305, Case No. 110.

24. Galveston **News**, 15th September, 1896; El Paso **Times**, 17th July, 1910.

25. Reeves County, Texas, Records, Case No. 238, **State of Texas vs Jim Miller;** Harkey, **Mean As Hell**, op. cit., p. 114.

26. Eastland County Records show that Miller was indicted in March, 1897, tried for the first time in June, 1897, and finally acquitted at his second trial in January, 1899.

27. Barney Riggs killed a man in Willcox, Arizona Territory, and was sentenced to life imprisonment in the Territorial Prison at Yuma. During an attempted jail break in October, 1887, he sided with the warders and killed a Mexican convict who was a member of a band of would-be escapers. It earned him a pardon and it was a macabre jest that he was the only man who had killed one man to get into prison and killed another one to get out. Details of the attempted crash-out and Riggs' actions are to be found in the **Tucson Citizen**, 5th November, 1887; also "Notes on an Interview with Hon. Thomas Gates," who was the prison Superintendent, in Eugene J. Trippel Papers, Arizona Pioneers' Historical Society Collection, Tucson.

28. Harkey, **Mean As hell**, op. cit., p. 73.

29. El Paso **Times**, 19th May, 1897.

30. He was killed there some years later by his step-son.

31. There is nothing known of this man to link him with Wyatt Earp and his brothers of Kansas and Arizona notoriety. He talked to that fantastic frontier journalist W.C. Brann, Editor of **The Iconoclast,** only a few minutes before Brann was killed by Captain Thomas E. Davis in Waco, Texas, on 2nd April, 1898 — **Brann and 'the Iconoclast'** by Charles Carver, (University of Texas Press, Austin, 1957; Thomas Nelson, London, 1958), p. 177.

32. Daniel R. "Dee" Harkey, one of twelve children, was born on 27th March, 1866, at Richland Springs, San Saba County, Texas. Several of his brothers were peace officers and Dee was in one law inforcement post or another virtually continuously from 1880 to 1911. He subsequently ranched in New Mexico and in 1948 published his reminiscences as a peace officer in frontier days under the title of **Mean As Hell**, op. cit., a controversial work much criticized by many old-time New Mexicans. He died at Carlsbad, New Mexico, on 18th June, 1958.

33. Harkey, **Mean As Hell**, op. cit., pp. 114-15; Judge James B. McGhee, interview with CR at Santa Fe, New Mexico, 9th October, 1967.

34. Harkey, **Mean As Hell**, op. cit., p. 115.

35. Ibid.
36. Ibid; also Keleher, **Fabulous Frontier,** op. cit., p. 80.
37. Sonnichsen, **Ten Texas Feuds,** op. cit., p. 207; Keleher, Fabulous Frontier, op. cit., p. 80; and Harkey, **Mean As Hell,** op. cit., p. 116.
38. Harkey, **Mean As Hell,** op. cit., p. 116; and Keleher, **Fabulous Frontier,** op. cit., p. 80.
39. Keleher, **Fabulous Frontier,** op. cit., p. 80.
40. Ibid.
41. **From Mustanger to Lawyer** by Max M. Coleman (Carleton Printing Co., San Antonio, 1953), Part B, p. 169; and Max M. Coleman, Lubbock, Texas, to CR, 6th April, 1959.
42. Keleher, **Fabulous Frontier,** op. cit., p. 80; Harkey, **Mean As Hell,** op. cit., pp. 115-16.

CHAPTER 4
DEATH ON THE LAS CRUCES ROAD

It was Oliver Lee who, according to Bill Isaacs, thought up the scheme which was used to goad Pat Garrett into a position in which he could be murdered and the deed made to appear as justifiable homicide.[1] Jim Miller preferred his business transactions carried out in an atmosphere where self-defense could be claimed, or where an assassination could be carried out with a shotgun blast from ambush in some isolated place. The intended murder of Garrett, however, presented two problems if it were to be done by ambush. Firstly, the region was reasonably thickly settled and for Miller to make a clean getaway after such a killing he would have needed a relay of horses, difficult to establish in complete secrecy. Secondly, Garrett was always on the watch. He had lived with danger for most of his adult life and it was known that when out riding he usually carried his Winchester rifle, not in his saddle bucket, but actually across the pommel,[2] where it could be used immediately if danger threatened.

Oliver Lee's solution, put to W.W. Cox, was to enrage Garrett so that he would make some kind of play which would get him killed. It had already been decided that he should be murdered on some lonely road by Jim Miller and that another man would take the blame for the killing. Carl Adamson was to be the necessary eye-witness to support the plea of self-defense, but first, for the benefit of the general public, Garrett had to be maneuvered into an untenable position, one which would give credence to the whole affair and be thought to have been Garrett's motive in getting into a gunfight.

Wayne Brazel, a Cox cowboy, had already been chosen as the man to take the blame for Garrett's death. He was known as a quiet young man, a non-drinker who had never been in serious trouble, who rarely carried a pistol except when riding the range,[3] and who could be relied upon to do Cox's bidding. He had already leased Garrett's Bear Canyon property — Cox may even have been paying the rent — and so was on the scene.

Jesse Wayne Brazel was his full name, though he never used the first name which had been his father's. Occasionally he appeared in official documents as J. Wayne Brazel,[4] but most people never knew that he had any other name than Wayne. He was not a particularly colorful character, nor even a particularly outstanding cowboy. History would not have recorded him, and he would have been no more than a memory to some of his old range buddies — except for one thing: he confessed to killing Pat Garrett, a man who was a living legend.

The Brazels were originally Wisconsin people, farmers who became stockmen, and fiddle-footed as was the way of the times. Robert Brazel, patriarch of the family, moved his brood to Verdigris, Kansas, in 1859, not an auspicious year to be in the midwest where the Abolitionists of "Bleeding Kansas" frequently clashed with the slave-holding Secessionists of Missouri. Old Robert's sons were William W."Bug," John, Marion and Jesse and when the War Between the States was little more than two years old John went away to fight. He joined the Sixth Cavalry at Fort Leavenworth in the spring of 1863.[5] There is some evidence that "Bug" also went to war, as a member of G Company, Ninth Kansas Cavalry, and in later years he was often referred to as "Captain." He also served as a county officer for a while.[6]

The Brazels were in Kansas for less than twenty years, long enough to put down roots, but not so long that they could not be pulled up. Some time in the late 1870s, probably the summer of 1877, they were on the move again, this time southward to Brown County, Texas. Old Robert, "Bug" and Marion seem to have pulled out first, to be joined later by Jesse and his wife and their new-born son Jesse Wayne. The baby was born on 31st December, 1877, and years later his range country friends remembered that he always celebrated twice as hard as anyone else on New Year's Eve.[7] The Brazels became cattlemen and at that period there was a gradual westward drift by many of the Texas stockmen. Old Robert and his son Marion went on a cattle drive to the Pecos country of New Mexico in 1879 and seem to have remained in the area for a short time.[8] Almost certainly they went back to Texas to bring the other members of the clan to the rolling rangelands of Eastern New Mexico, which are really part of the Llano Estacado which belongs to Texas.

Some time in 1881 the Brazel family moved into New Mexico and soon filed on public land on Eagle Creek in Lincoln County. This time they settled down and stayed. Possibly they retained land in Texas, for Old Robert was in that State when he died in 1884. W.W. Brazel was to figure in an unofficial census of Union veterans, compiled in 1893, as having first come to New Mexico with the Army and to have mustered out of the service at Fort Stanton in 1863, though there is no official confirmation of this. The family of Jesse Brazel — wife and two sons, Wayne and Rothmer — were supported by their father's labor at the Mormon gold mines. Eventually he was killed in an accident and lies buried beside his brother "Bug" at Gold Camp, a now deserted settlement within the area of the White Sands Missile Base where the first atomic bomb was exploded.[9]

Wayne Brazel was nineteen years old on New Year's Eve, 1896, and was already working as a cowboy for W.W. Cox, whose feuding and shooting days were far behind him and who was now a prosperous rancher in the Western Tularosa Basin.

Bert Judia, who was foreman at Cox's San Augustine Ranch at Organ Gap in 1908 and knew Wayne Brazel as a hard-working cowboy there, called him "a quiet, fine young man, with an excellent record." He was, so Judia believed, "mild and inoffensive,"[10] and Lorenzo D. Walters, who knew him just after the turn of the century, considered him to be "a good natured, slow moving cowboy."[11]

John Milton Scanland, an intinerant newspaperman who also knew Brazel, set down a physical description of him.

"Brazel is a typical cowboy in appearance, and to emphasize it, wears a black broad-rimmed hat, the crown pushed up high, and the hat pulled well over his ears," he wrote. "He is 31 years of age and is unmarried. He has a ruddy complexion, sandy hair, rough features, is strongly built, and is smooth shaven. He has a scar reaching from the right corner of his mouth over his chin, evidently a wound from a knife."[12]

It is known that he idolized W.W. Cox and while most of the Cox cowhands, with the almost feudal loyalty of the real range man to his employer would have faced flaming guns and considered it no more than in the line of duty, young Wayne Brazel would undoubtedly have gone even further if the occasion demanded it. Jarvis P. Garrett — and, as Brazel admitted killing Pat Garrett, Jarvis cannot be considered a completely impartial witness — probably summed Wayne up as well as anyone who had less reason to be prejudiced against him when he said: "He would follow instructions to the letter, he knew how to keep his mouth shut, and he could be used as a front man. He was a perfect tool for the conspiracy."[13]

Soon after Thanksgiving Day 1907 Brazel began acquiring small herds of goats and driving them to the Bear Canyon property he was renting. In January, 1908, he bought a large herd and drove them to the pasturage and turned them loose. The result was almost immediate. Pat Garrett learned that his ranch was being used for goats and flew into a rage, reacting as he had been expected to react, as any cattleman would have reacted. Goats were as bad, if not worse, than sheep to a cattleman's way of thinking. They grazed the grass almost down to the roots, often worrying it out of the ground in their efforts to get every little bit of nutriment. After sheep or goats had grazed a range it was unfit for cattle, who do not crop as much, for at least a season, often more.

"Garrett's immediate reaction to this provocative act was hostile, because he felt that Brazel had acted in bad faith," Jarvis P. Garrett wrote. His anger was all the greater because "there was nothing he could do about it in accordance with the terms of the contract, which did not specify that goats were excluded."[14]

Garrett maintained that when the ranch had been leased Brazel had said that he intended to run between three and four hundred head of cattle on the property. Brazel insisted that he had said nothing about the kind of stock he intended to graze at Bear Canyon. Garrett thought it over for a while and then had Brazel hauled before a Justice of the Peace under an old Territorial statute which made it an offense to herd stock within a mile-and-a half of a ranch house or settlement, but the case was thrown out of court.[15]

The plotters left Garrett to fume and fuss for a while and then sent Carl Adamson to see him. It was the end of the first week in February and Adamson presented himself as the partner of James P. Miller, wealthy Oklahoma cattleman. He explained that Miller was having a thousand head of Mexican cattle delivered at El Paso on 15th March and that he wanted them to spend the summer fattening up on New Mexican grass before being moved to Miller's ranch in Oklahoma in the fall. Adamson said that he had seen the Bear Canyon property and considered it an ideal place for the purpose. He would like to take a lease on it, he told Garrett, and would pay a stated sum per head of cattle put onto the property.[16] There also seems to have been some discussion about the sale of the ranch, with the figure of $3,000 being named.[17]

The deal sounded good to Garrett, too good, in fact, to be allowed to slip through his fingers. There was only one snag: Wayne Brazel's goats. Garrett told Adamson that he "would have to get a goat man off first"[18] and Adamson went to El Paso, where Jim Miller was waiting for news, and informed him that things were going according to plan. Garrett, meanwhile, asked Brazel to cancel his contract, which Brazel said he was willing to do, providing that he could sell the twelve hundred head of goats at Bear Canyon. A meeting at Las Cruces between Garrett, Miller, Adamson and Brazel was arranged[19] and Miller said that he was willing to pay $3.50 a head for the twelve hundred goats which Brazel said he had. Brazel then agreed to surrender the lease of the property.[20] Garrett was exultant. He had never hoped for such a solution. He met Brazel in Las Cruces a few days later and told him that everything was arranged. He was awaiting news from Miller and Adamson, who had returned to El Paso, about clinching the deal. Brazel apparently told Garrett that he thought there might now be more than twelve hundred goats as they had been kidding. Garrett flew into a rage when Brazel added that as far as he was concerned the deal had to cover the sale of all his goats, or else he would sell none of them and would stay on the Bear Canyon property. There were hard words. Those who were bent on stirring up trouble, put it around that Garrett had slapped Brazel's face.[21]

At about this time something happened which may or may have been connected with subsequent events. One night in mid-February an employee of Garrett's named Frank Adams was awakened by the sound of somebody moving about in the darkness near the ranch buildings. He saw the shadowy figures of two men sneaking up to the house. Quietly he woke Garrett, but his employer refused to belive that there was anyone outside and told Adams that the noise must have been made by dogs. The following morning, however, they found the clearly defined footprints of two men just where Adams said he had seen the intruders, and in a nearby ravine they found tracks where two horses had been tethered. [22] It made Garrett jittery and he sent word to Governor George Curry that he was expecting trouble. [23] He was unable to suggest what form it might take, but commented that "if he did not get them, they would get him," or so newspaper reporter John Scanland was told. [24] According to Scanland, who made his investigation less than a month later, Curry was deeply disturbed by Garrett's message, for he knew that his old friend did not worry without good cause. He decided to send some members of the Territorial Mounted Police into the Organ Mountains country, but events overtook him. [25]

Garrett, in the meantime, had decided to see if he could take legal action against Wayne Brazel, just in case the deal to lease or sell the ranch fell through because of Brazel's intransigence, and the fact that there now appeared to be half as many goats again as had been originally discussed. He visited El Paso — where he received a letter threatening him with death — and discussed the matter with a lawyer, [26] but what advice he received was never revealed.

Badly in need of funds to tide him over until the Bear Canyon business was concluded, Garrett sent an urgent note to Curry, who was still paying off his debt piecemeal. It read "Dear Curry: I am in a hell of a fix. I have been trying to sell my ranch but no luck. For God's sake send me fifty dollars." [27] A check arrived almost by return of post.

Adamson returned to Las Cruces with the news that Miller was to come up from El Paso to finalize the deal the following day. Garrett at once offered Adamson the hospitality of his home for the night, saying that they could drive into Las Cruces the following morning, meet Miller and Brazel there and sign the necessary papers. Adamson said that he had some business affairs to attend to in town that afternoon and would join Garrett at his home in the early evening. Garrett went back to have his wife prepare for their guest and sent a note to Wayne Brazel's home. He was not there, but the envelope was sent on to the Organ Gap ranch. Brazel was shoeing horses with foreman Bert Judia when it arrived. [28]

Adamson, meanwhile, got busy on the Western Union telegraph

lines. It was subsequently learned that a series of telegrams were filed that afternoon by and between Carl Adamson, Jim Miller, Wayne Brazel, W.W. Cox and "Print" Rhode.[29] After concluding his business with the telegraph company Adamson rode out to Garrett's ranch to spend the night. During the evening Wayne Brazel arrived with a note for Adamson. Its content was never disclosed, but the Garrett family subsequently concluded that it was to give Adamson his final instructions.[30]

The same evening Jim Miller left El Paso quietly and headed for a ranch in Southeastern New Mexico owned by Judge Charles R. Brice and lawman "Dee" Harkey, both of whom he knew well, and who were not living on the premises. The foreman was Joe Beasley, the man Miller had tried to use Joe Earp to frame in Collingsworth County, Texas, for the reward offered for a murderer. Either Beasley had a short memory, which does not seem likely, or he was mortally afraid of Miller, which is highly probable. "Killing Jim" told Beasley that he was going to take one of the best horses at the ranch and ride over into Dona Ana County to kill Pat Garrett. He warned that in the unlikely event of him being charged with the murder he would expect Beasley to provide testimony to show that he had never left the Harkey-Brice ranch.[31] The spot where the killing was to be done had already been selected and Miller rode all night to be in position soon after first light.

On the morning of 29th February, 1908, Garrett and Adamson made ready for the four-hour drive to Las Cruces. Up at the Cox ranch at Organ Gap young Wayne Brazel was also preparing for the trip.

"There was a horse in the remuda they called 'Loco' because he went crazy when he heard a gun click," Bert Judia, who saw Brazel ride away, said later. "This horse must have been powder-burned at some time, because he was deathly afraid of anything connected with firearms. It was a cold morning and Wayne was wearing a canvas coat lined with sheepskin and he had it buttoned."[32]

'Loco' was the horse selected by Wayne Brazel that fateful morning. Ironically, the animal had belonged to the young man Reed who was killed back in 1899 by Jose Espalin when he, Garrett and the Oklahoma peace officer went to the ranch to make an inquiry.

At the Garrett ranch the two men prepared to leave.

"Garrett held the reins in his gloved hands, and Adamson sat at his side on the buckboard," Jarvis P. Garrett wrote. "At the moment of departure, Garrett asked that he be handed his shotgun, saying he would get some birds on the way back. The shotgun was a 10-gauge, the barrels were detached, and together with the stock fitted into a leather case. The gun had to be assembled before it could be used. As Frank Adams, an employee of the ranch, handed him the shotgun, he asked Garrett if he wanted his pistol. Adamson was quick to suggest that it wouldn't be needed. No sooner had they left than Mrs. Garrett noticed that her husband had forgotten to take his overcoat. She gave it to her daughter, Pauline, who mounted her horse and galloped in pursuit. She caught up with the two men at the entrance gate to the ranch. She was the last member of the family to see Garrett alive. She remained at the gate, watching the buggy (sic) as it drew out of sight, and as she was about to return to the ranch, observed a man on horseback riding in the same direction. It was Wayne Brazel."[33]

Adamson claimed later that as Garrett took the gun he said: "I'll place this between us, because we may have trouble before we get to town."[34]

The buckboard traveled slowly and after some time Wayne Brazel caught up with it. He had a Winchester in his saddle boot and a pistol on his left hip.[35] The old argument about Brazel having brought in the goats in the first place was gone through all over again. Brazel told Garrett that he was now certain that he had considerably more goats than Adamson and Miller had agreed to buy. Maybe as many as eighteen hundred. It was a bombshell to Garrett, more so when Adamson chipped in to say that if there were that many he thought he would have to cancel the whole deal. There were strong words on both sides.

They reached the little settlement of Organ and stopped briefly at L.C. Bentley's general store and post office. Bentley subsequently reported that Garrett looked angry and that the argument began again as they left for Las Cruces. He said that he heard Brazel say: "But Pat, I can't get those goats off."[36]

The buckboard and Brazel, who rode with his right side towards the vehicle,[37] crossed the mesa, open country where a man could see for miles, and entered a series of low foothills, on the far side of which lay Las Cruces. The country was broken, with black, wind-blown, stunted brush beside the trail, half-starved vegetation trying to grow despite the poor sandy soil and the endless winds.

Carl Adamson knew the spot which had been chosen for the killing and as they neared it he began to fidget. He told Garrett that he wanted to get out of the buckboard to relieve himself. Garrett reined in and both he and Adamson alighted. Garrett decided to relieve himself, too, and went to the edge of the road, turning his back on the buckboard and the two men. Adamson went to the horses' heads and held them to stop them from bolting at the sound of the gunfire he knew was coming. Garrett's folding shotgun lay on the seat where he had left it and he slipped off his left-hand driving glove and undid his flies.

Up the road a piece, hidden in the scrub, Jim Miller got the back of the old gray head in the sights of his rifle and squeezed the trigger.

The first shot cracked out and Miller's marksmanship was precise. Pat Garrett jerked forward as the bullet smashed into the back of his head. He spun round and began to fall backwards into a sand drift by the roadside. Miller levered another shell into his Winchester and fired again at the falling man. The bullet caught Garrett in the region of the stomach and ranged upwards. He moaned and writhed on his back for a moment and then he was dead. The first shot had done the main work, a ghastly wound over his right eye showing where the bullet had come out.

Garrett's shotgun, still not assembled, was taken from the buckboard by Adamson and put in the sand near its late owner's outstretched hand. Then he spread a lap robe over the body and climbed back into the buckboard. Wayne Brazel, after tying his horse to the tailboard, joined Adamson in the driving seat and they jigged the horses and drove away. They passed the spot where Jim Miller had lain in ambush, his horse making tracks which would puzzle investigators, but the hired gunman was already on his way, racing his mount from the scene of the shooting to keep to the time schedule necessary for his alibi.

Shortly after noon Wayne Brazel and Adamson drove up to Henry Stoes' house in Las Cruces and called him out from his lunch.

"I just killed Pat Garrett," Brazel told Stoes. "He's lying under a lap robe about five miles out. I had to do it. It was him or me. Will you come to the Sheriff's Office?"[38]

The three men went down to the office of Deputy Sheriff Felipe Lucero[39] of Dona Ana County and there Brazel surrendered himself.

"I was getting ready to go to lunch when the door to the Sheriff's Office opened and in walked Wayne Brazel, looking hurried and upset," Lucero said later. "He had a gun in his hand, and as he came up to my desk he laid it down in front of me. 'Lock me up . . . I've just killed Pat Garrett,' he said. I laughed at him saying, 'What are you trying to do, Wayne, josh me?' But he insisted he'd just killed Pat Garret with his .45 on the Organ road. I gave him a second look and saw he wasn't joking. I put his gun into the safe and locked him up in a cell.

"I put his horse into the stable where we kept our mounts, and untied my own. Already Wayne had told me where I'd find Pat Garrett, lying dead in a sandy arroyo about four miles east of town. 'The man who was with Pat when I killed him,' Wayne had told me, 'is outside the jail sitting in Pat's buggy. He's a man named Adamson and he saw the whole thing and knows I shot in self-defense.' Sure enough, I found this Adamson waiting for me. He followed me while I summoned a coroner's jury, and then trailed along behind when I led the way to the scene of the shooting."[40]

Lucero took with him Dr. W.C. Field[41] and they made independent investigations of the condition of the body and the place where the crime had occurred. Then Pat Garrett's long frame was lifted onto a spring wagon driven by Clarence Snook[42] and taken back to Las Cruces. The Garrett family was notified at once and they, in turn, sent word to relatives.

The news of Pat Garrett's death shocked New Mexico, indeed the entire Southwest, for he was one of the best-known of Western range men. Hundreds of letters and telegrams of sympathy poured into the Garrett home, including one from Theodore Roosevelt[43] and another from the old lawman's long-time friend, the Western author Emerson Hough.[44]

Among the letters, significantly, was one with an El Paso postmark addressed to Garrett's crippled son, Dudley. It warned that he, too might be murdered[45] and stated: "Brazel shot Garrett from the back and that another shot him from the front." The letter concluded: "Hanging without trial is what Brazel should get." It was signed: "One who knows."[46]

There was no coffin in Las Cruces long enough for Garrett's six-foot-four-inch frame and a telegram was sent to El Paso for assistance. An undertaker there was able to supply a suitable casket and hurried northward with it.[47] The body lay in state at the Strong Undertaking Parlors and scores of people filed past to take a final look at the man who had killed Billy the Kid and turned a small-time local hoodlum into a national legend. Pat Garrett's brothers John and Alfred arrived from Louisiana.

The funeral took place at three o'clock on the afternoon of 5th March at the Odd Fellows' Cemetery in Las Cruces. The pallbearers were George Curry, Harry Lane, Morgan Llewellyn, Numa G. Buchoz and Tom Powers.[48] The grave had been dug in the northwest corner, next to that of Garrett's daughter Ida who had died eight years earlier. He had been a Free Thinker, an agnostic, a disciple, inasmuch as he ever thought about it, of Robert Green Ingersoll, and had not wanted a religious service at his funeral. As the coffin was lowered Tom Powers read from the eulogy delivered by Ingersoll at the graveside of his own brother.

"Life is a narrow vale between the cold and barren peaks of two eternities," Powers intoned to the over-sized casket and the tight-lipped throng of people at the open grave. "We strive in vain to look beyond the heights. We cry aloud — and the only answer is the echo of our wailing cry. From the voiceless lips of the unreplying dead there comes no word. But in the night of death Hope sees a star and listening love can hear the rustle of a wing."[49]

NOTES
CHAPTER 4

1. Sonnichsen, **Tularosa,** op. cit., p. 319, quoting an interview with Bill Isaacs of Las Cruces, 15th September, 1954, says that Cox called in Oliver Lee for advice about getting Garrett off his property and Lee suggested that they "goat him off."
2. Burt Judia, art, cit., p. 46.
3. Ibid., p. 47; also **Tombstone's Yesterday** by Lorenzo D. Walters (Acme Printing Co., Tucson, 1928), p. 121. Walter's book is frequently inaccurate, mostly when he speaks of things he heard or thought he heard. However, when dealing with matters about which he had personal knowledge he is far more reliable. He knew both Garrett and Brazel at the turn of the century and substantiates Judia's statement when he says that Brazel was "Never in the habit of going armed," except when out riding; certainly never in town.
4. The name Brazel has been spelled in various ways, the most usual alternative being Brazil. Robert N. Mullin has collected a great deal of material on the family and asserts that the correct spelling seems to be Brazel. He has had the advantage of interviewing a number of members of the family who spell their name in this manner. Mr. Mullin writes: "The variations in spelling by the census records, the newspapers, etc., lend some confusion: Brasle, Brazil, Brazel, Brassell, etc. One of the present generation spells his name Brazil, though legal documents in my possession indicate that Wayne's father and other relatives spelled the name Brazel" — Robert N. Mullin, South Laguna, California, to CR, 1st April, 1965. The spelling Brazel will by used throughout, except where, in quoted material, it is spelled otherwise. Wayne Brazel appeared officially as "J. Wayne Brazel," for example, in a court case involving the forgery of a homestead claim — Santa Fe **New Mexican,** 11th November, 1914.
5. Family history concerning the Brazels in Greenwood County, Kansas, is contained in "Some Lost Towns of Kansas — Greenwood City" by Edwin Walters, of Kansas City, Missouri **(Kansas Historical Collections,** Volume XII, 1911-1912), pp. 29-30.
6. An unofficial census of Union soldiers in the Civil War, taken in New Mexico in 1893, gives W.W. Brazel's date of enlistment as 1st November, 1861. If this record is correct, which it very possibly is not, he must either have been on leave, or have been elected by proxy, when the County Convention was held at William Ott's farm in August, 1862. He was selected as a County Officer. The same unofficial census states that he was serving "in the field" at Fort Stanton, New Mexico, in 1863 and received his discharge from the service there. However, Federal and Territorial official military records fail to reveal any William W. Brazel serving with the Army —

Robert N. Mullin to CR, 19th April, 1965, and 8th October, 1966.

7. Bill McCall, old-time cowboy and friend of Wayne Brazel, to Robert N. Mullin in an interview in April, 1964 — Robert N. Mullin to CR, 19th April, 1965. Mr. Mullin reports that Mrs. Clara Snow, grand-daughter of W.W. Brazel, "believes, but isn't sure, that her grandfather didn't move from Kansas until 1878 or 1879."

8. Robert N. Mullin to CR, 1st April, 1965. Exhaustive research by Mr. Mullin has failed to reveal any family links with M.S. Brazil, who had a ranch northeast of Fort Sumner in 1880 and co-operated with Pat Garrett in the search for Billy the Kid's rustler band. Nor does the family appear to be connected with Manuel Brazil, who had a spread near Bosque Grande, or one Moody Brazil, who ranched in Lincoln County, New Mexico, in the late 1880s. Wayne Brazel said in 1908 that he knew Garrett "20 years ago" when they both lived in Lincoln County — Scanland, op. cit., p. 9.

9. "Greenwood City" by Edwin Walters, art. cit., p. 29. There is some dispute about the date of the deaths of both Jesse and W.W. Brazel. Edwin Walters, p. 30, says that W.W. Died in 1889 and Jesse in 1904. Mrs. Snow told Robert N. Mullin that her grandfather died "about 1890," but an old Cox Ranch cowboy told him it was about 1893 — adding 'I ought to know, because I was at the funeral." Nick Carter, an old Otero County resident, said that Jesse died in 1890, though it is possible that he was confusing Jesse with W.W. The Las Cruces newspapers offer no help as regards the death of either man. In 1964 Mr. Mullin flew to Gold Camp (later known as Mormon Gold Camp) by helicopter, accompanied by the Commanding General of the Missile Range, but the results of the trip were disappointing. "The original grave markers are all gone, or so rotted as to be illegible," Mr. Mullin reported. "On one of the headstones a metal plate reads: Cap't W.W. Brazel, Sarah J. Brazel, Jesse M. Brazel, 1892. The 1892 date must have been established by guesswork, as the metal plate was affixed many years later by surviving members of the family, according to one of the present generation of Brazels" — Robert N. Mullin to CR, 19th April, 1965.

10. Bert Judia, art. cit., p. 47. Judia has told pretty much the same thing to other researchers — Robert N. Mullin to CR, 1st and 19th April, 1965.

11. Lorenzo D. Walters, op. cit., p. 121. Old-time U.S. Line Rider Kenneth Oliver called Brazel "just a big old good-natured cowpuncher and a nice fellow" — "Foot-Loose and Fancy Free' by Kenneth Oliver as told to Jane Pattie (**Old West,** Volume Six, Number 2, Whole Number 22, Winter, 1969), p. 5.

12. Scanland, op. cit., pp. 8-9.

13. Jarvis P. Garrett, op. cit., p. 41.

14. Ibid., p. 42.

15. Scanland, op. cit., p. 4.

16. Keleher, **Fabulous Frontier,** op. cit., p. 76; Sonnichsen, **Tularosa,** op. cit., p. 230 and p. 238, seems to indicate that Adamson rather than Miller did all the negotiating and that Garrett did not actually meet Miller. Wayne Brazel, at his trial, however, consistently referred to things he said Garrett

had told him that Miller had said, and Jarvis P. Garrett, op. cit., p. 42, says that his father had direct negotiations on at least one occasion with Miller who "appeared to be the spokesman" — a fact consistent with the whole fabrication that Miller had an Oklahoma ranch and that Adamson was his partner. Scanland, op. cit., p. 4, confirms this.

17. Scanland, op. cit., p. 5; George Curry, **Autobiography,** op. cit., p. 217, also refers to the fact that an actual sale of the ranch was discussed.

18. Ibid.

19. Testimony of Carl Adamson, El Paso **Daily Herald,** 5th March, 1908.

20. Scanland, op. cit., p. 5.

21. George Curry, **Autobiography,** op. cit., p. 217. This face-slapping story was challenged when Curry's book came out.

22. Scanland, op. cit., p. 11.

23. Ibid., p. 8.

24. Ibid.

25. Ibid., pp. 10-11.

26. Ibid., p. 5.

27. This tends to confirm Scanland's statement that Garrett had discussed the selling of the ranch with Miller and Brazel, as well as the possible leasing of the property. Jarvis P. Garrett, op. cit., p. 41, mentions this letter from Garrett to Curry, and the fact that it brought a check by return post, and complains that it has in the past been suggested that it was merely Curry's generous spirit which moved him to send the check to his old friend. Jarvis says that this is not the case. The money was part of that owed to Garrett.

28. Bert Judia, art. cit., p. 47.

29. Reference was made to these telegrams prior to Brazel's trial, but they were not produced at it — Keleher, **Fabulous Frontier,** op. cit., p. 76.

30. Jarvis P. Garrett, op. cit., pp. 42-43.

31. Harkey, **Mean As Hell,** op. cit., p. 116.

32. Bert Judia, art. cit., p. 47.

33. Jarvis P. Garrett, op. cit., p. 43. It has been said that the Organ Gap ranch "was within spy-glass distance of the Garrett ranch" — Ibid., p. 41, but unless the land has changed considerably such a spy-glass would have to be capable of seeing through sand hills.

34. Scanland, op. cit., p. 5.

35. Ibid.

36. Sonnichsen, **Tularosa,** op. cit., p. 238, quoting an interview with L.C. Bentley at Organ on 7th November, 1953.

37. Scanland, op. cit., p. 5.

38. Ibid., p. 238.

39. Felipe Lucero was born in 1867 in Dona Ana County, New Mexico, and spent his whole life there. His father, a farmer and stockraiser who also engaged in merchandising, had migrated from Chihuahua, Mexico, in 1859. Felipe was appointed a Deputy Sheriff in 1901, serving under his brother, and in 1909 he ran for election and became Sheriff. After a long and useful life devoted to community service he died in 1940 and was

buried at the Masonic Cemetery at Las Cruces, New Mexico, on 1st August — Robert N. Mullin to CR, 8th May, 1968.

40. **New Mexico Sentinel,** 23rd April, 1939, giving former Sheriff Felipe Lucero's account of the Garrett killing. The same issue carried the reminiscences of Dr. W.C. Field, the attending physician.

41. William C. Field, 1863-1947, was born in Nova Scotia and reached New Mexico in 1905 from California. He practiced medicine in Las Cruces until his death on 22nd December, 1947. He was buried in the Masonic Cemetery at Las Cruces — Las Cruces **Sun News,** 23rd December, 1947; also Robert N. Mullin to CR, 15th May, 1968.

42. Clarence Snook, of Lebanon, Ohio, to CR, 20th May, 1965.

43. El Paso **Daily Herald,** 3rd March, 1908.

44. Emerson Hough was born in Newton, Iowa, on 28th June, 1857. In 1883 he set himself up as a lawyer in White Oaks, New Mexico, but after a year found that he had little interest in the profession. He had written articles for the town's newspaper the **Golden Era** and in 1884 returned to Iowa and engaged in newspaper work. Later he turned to novels, drawing much of his material from real-life incidents and characters he had met in his New Mexican sojourn. Among his books were **The Way of the West, Heart's Desire, The Covered Wagon, The Story of the Cowboy, Fifty-Four Forty or Fight** and **North of 36.** He had been especially friendly with Pat Garrett and in 1904 returned to New Mexico and traveled extensively with Garrett gathering material for **The Story of the Outlaw.** He also wrote many short stories and a number of biographical sketches of frontier characters. He died in Chicago on 30th April, 1923.

45. Sonnichsen, **Tularosa,** op. cit., p. 319.

46. Scanland, op. cit., p. 11.

47. Martin, **Border Boss,** op. cit., p. 151.

48. Scanland, op. cit. p. 1.

49. Jarvis P. Garrett, op. cit., p. 47. He adds that after the Odd Fellows' Cemetery was abandoned some vandals destroyed Ida's tombstone, and in the fall of 1957 he and his sister Pauline arranged for the remains of their father and sister to be reinterred across the road in the Masonic Cemetery; also Sonnichsen, **Tularosa,** op. cit., pp. 242-43; Keleher, **Fabulous Frontier,** op. cit., pp. 74-75; and El Paso **Daily Herald,** 3rd March, 1908.

Pat Garrett

W.W. Cox

Albert B. Fall

The Conspirators

Oliver Lee

Mannie Clements

The Assassin

Jim Miller (above) got away with the murder of Pat Garrett, but he was not so lucky on his next assignment as a gun for hire and was lynched (below) at Ada, Oklahoma. Left to right: Jim Miller, Joe Allen, B.B. Burwell, Jesse West.

George Curry

James M. Hervey

the Investigators

Fred Fornoff

Rare photo of Wayne Brazel (seated, center). Believed taken about 1906, after a visit to the barber, and said not to be a good likeness.

Grave of Pat Garrett

CHAPTER 5
INVESTIGATION AND TRIAL

Many years after Garrett's death former Deputy Sheriff Felipe Lucero recalled what was found when he, along with Dr. W.C. Field, the spring-wagon driver Clarence Snook and the members of the coroner's jury, reached the scene of the murder.

The dead man, Lucero said, was "lying flat on his back, one leg drawn up, his gun lying near him. We could plainly see the wheel tracks of the buggy and the impression of the horses' hooves in the sand, the depressions they'd made when they plunged at the sounds of the shots. I trailed the tracks back for about two miles and saw where the horse Wayne Brazel had been riding joined the buggy at the old chalk hill. It was plain to see that the team and the horse had been walked side by side, the men apparently talking together as they rode." [1]

Dr. W.C. Field, a skilled physician and an observant one too, carried out a detailed search of both the body and the murder spot.

"I made a careful physical examination of the body," he said much later. "Pat had been shot twice, once in the head, once in the body. He was lying flat on his back, one knee drawn up. His clothes were open and disarranged, showing that he gotten from the buggy to relieve himself at the time he was killed. He'd taken the glove from his left hand, but a heavy driving glove was still on his right hand. I couldn't help but ponder on that point.

"A man as wise in such matters as Pat wouldn't have kept his glove on, wouldn't have been in the position he had probably been in, wouldn't have turned his back if he'd thought he was in any physical danger . . . Pat's gun lay parallel to his body about three feet from under him. It was a shotgun, the kind he generally carried, broken and in its scabbard. It lay without any sand kicked up around it. That was another point I noticed. When a man's shot in the back of the head, the way Pat was, he does one of two things with whatever he has in his hand. Either he clutches it convulsively tight or he throws it wide. Threre were no signs in the sand that the gun had been violently thrown." [2]

Walking around observing tracks and markings, Dr. Field also stumbled across the place where Jim Miller had waited patiently for his victim. There was fresh manure and the ground was trampled down where the horse had moved around during the vigil beside the trail.

"Later at the undertaking parlor I made an autopsy on Pat," Dr. Field added. "He'd been shot twice by soft nosed bullets from a .45, one shot hitting him in the back of the head and emerging just over the right eye. The second shot was fired when Pat was nearly on the ground, the bullet striking in the region of the stomach and ranging upward. I cut this bullet out behind the shoulder. I was sure he'd been shot in the back of the head because when I examined the hole I noticed it was driven inward toward the wound."[3]

Carl Adamson gave his initial version of the murder to the coroner's jury.

"We stopped to urinate," he said. "Wayne Brazel and Pat Garrett started to argue. Pat Garrett was getting out of the buggy with a shotgun in his hand. Wayne Brazel shot him. I didn't see how it all happened."[4]

Dudley Poe Garrett, the dead man's eldest son, officially charged Wayne Brazel with murder two days after the killing.[5]

George Curry had not gone to the funeral at Las Cruces alone. After receiving a telegram giving details of Garrett's murder he had left Santa Fe, taking with him Captain Fred Fornoff[6] of the Territorial Mounted Police and Attorney-General James Madison Hervey.[7]

"He came to me soon after the news of Garrett's murder was out and said that he would go down to Las Cruces the next day to the funeral and suggested that I go along, as the talk was running pretty high among Garrett's friends and there might be trouble," James M. Hervey recalled. "It had gotten out that Albert B. Fall had been retained to defend Brazel and that the district attorney was a pretty close friend of Fall's. He thought there should be an independent investigation."[8]

While Curry went to Pat Garrett's funeral Hervey and Fred Fornoff drove out to the scene of the murder with Carl Adamson. They stopped their buckboard exactly where Garrett had stopped his and listened to Adamson's version of what had happened. It was substantially as he had testified at the preliminary hearing. Hervey left Fornoff and Adamson talking and began prowling around by himself. In due course as he put it, "I happened to spy a new Winchester rifle shell on the ground."[9] A second shell case was found by Fornoff nearby.

When Hervey heard Brazel's story a few days later he noticed not only discrepancies between it and the Adamson version, but between it and the evidence of his own eyes at the murder spot. He began asking questions about Brazel and the answers he got only served to strengthen his suspicions. "Brazel had never been considered a dangerous man,"[10] he said. "And anyway, Garrett would not make such a fool play."[11] George Curry had done some questioning of his own about the self-confessed killer. "From all I could learn, Brazel was a quiet young man and not of the killer type," he said later.[12]

On 3rd March a preliminary hearing against Wayne Brazel was held in the court of Justice of the Peace Manuel Lopez.

"The prisoner, Wayne Brazel, was accompanied in the courtroom by his friend, W.W. Cox, his constant companion before the tragedy," reporter John Scanland, who was present, wrote later. "Cox is not related to Brazel, but they had always been 'close friends.' Brazel occupied the prisoner's chair, facing the justice, and seemed nervous and ill at ease. The two attorneys for the defense sat at the right. Attorney-General J.M. Hervey, who had charge of the prosecution, sat to the left of the prisoner. A few feet distant sat Dudley Poe Garrett and his sisters, Elizabeth and Annie." [13]

Carl Adamson testified first.

"I knew Pat Garrett about three weeks," he said. "Brazel, I met about a week ago. On our way in that morning, just the other side of Organ, we saw Brazel talking to someone in the road. [14] He passed us on horseback — had a Winchester on his saddle. We only spoke. No, we didn't exactly travel together. Sometimes he was close, sometimes he was behind.

"When we were getting close to Las Cruces I asked him if his goats were kidding. Garrett said, 'How does it come you signed a contract for twelve hundred goats when you've got eighteen hundred?' 'Well,' I said, 'I don't know if we want eighteen hundred goats or not. We might break up the deal. I didn't want the twelve hundred, but I bought them to get possession of the ranch.' 'If I don't sell the whole bunch, I won't sell none,' Brazel says. 'If I have to keep any goats I'll stay on the ranch.'

"Pat got pretty mad at that. 'I don't care whether you give up the ranch or not. I can get you off anyway.' 'I don't know whether you can or not,' [said Brazel]. About that time I got out to relieve myself. Garrett took the lines. I heard him say, 'Damn you, I'll get you off now.' He was starting to get out of the buggy with his shotgun in his hand when Brazel shot him. He staggered back and fell. He stretched and groaned a little after he fell, and that was all. I took the lap robe and covered him up, and we came on in. Brazel gave me his six-shooter." [15]

The three Territorial officials returned to Santa Fe and discussed the affair. Curry had learned that Garrett had been carrying shells for the shotgun loaded with birdshot, not heavy duty shells, which he felt indicated "that he had not been expecting trouble." [16] Fornoff and the Attorney-General agreed that, as Hervey put it, "there was something wrong about the story." [17] Curry, setting down his memories of the case some years later, referred to the "mysterious circumstances surrounding the killing." [18] He had obviously heard rumors around Las Cruces, and had learned that his check for $50 was found in Garrett's pocket, still uncashed. [19] The suspicions held by Fornoff and Hervey, he said, "confirmed the impression from some of the information I had obtained, that Brazel was the victim of a conspiracy rather than the killer, an impression that later became a firm belief."[20]

Curry was shocked to find Garrett doing business with men like Jim Miller and Carl Adamson and said so — "It was difficult for me to understand why Garrett would enter into any kind of business deal with such men, as he knew their records"[21] — showing how little he really understood the lengths to which Garrett had been driven by his financial plight.

Hervey and Fornoff decided that the only way to find out what had really happened would be to have a detective in the area who could move around and listen to the gossip and hear what was being said, but the Territory of New Mexico had no funds at the time to employ such a man.[22]

"A month or so later I had business in El Paso, where Garrett had spent a good deal of time, and found out who some of his friends were," James M. Hervey recalled. "One was Tom Powers, who was owner of the Coney Island Saloon and pretty well-to-do; another was a Dr. Culinan. I took a personal interest in this matter because Garrett had been a friend of my father and if he had been murdered I thought the guilty should be prosecuted. I told these two friends about my suspicions and told them that if we had the money to put a detective in that country for a few months, under cover, that it would be revealed whether my suspicions were well founded, but they did not seem to want to put up any money."[23]

The Territorial Press had not been slow to question the whole affair either.

The day after the funeral the Capitan **News** remarked that the Brazel-Adamson version of the killing had been "received with a great deal of incredulity." As the first shot had struck Garrett in the back if the head, the paper said, the second shot "could have been fired only when the body was prone on the ground; for the bullet struck near the fourth rib, ranged upward and lodged in the shoulder."[24]

In early April it suddenly became known that the itinerant newspaperman John Scanland,[25] who had been busy interviewing people left, right and center for the past month, was collecting material for a book on the life and death of Pat Garrett. The news was warmly received in some quarters, and in others it caused a certain amount of concern.

Scanland's talks with Carl Adamson produced a somewhat different story from the one the eye-witness had given in court.

"Adamson said in an interview that he got out of the buggy to fix the harness, and that while standing beside the buggy, he heard Garrett say to Brazel, 'I don't give a —— whether you sell all your goats and give up the lease, or not. I can get you off anyway; I'll put you out right now.' Garrett then leaped from the buggy, Adamson says, 'but I don't know whether he grabbed his gun as he did so, or whether he got his gun later — after Brazel had shot and before he fell. I did not see as I was on the other side of the horse. I know that when Garrett fell he dropped his gun, and it had not been fired. It was a folding pump gun, and loaded with bird shot. I am sure that Garrett did not know that Brazel had a revolver. He saw Brazel's Winchester strapped beside him on the horse, and had his eye on that. I am sure he thought he could cover Brazel with his shotgun before Brazel could draw the Winchester and so he did not count on Brazel's revolver, as he did not know that he had one. As Garrett fell to the ground he was dead. There were two bullets in his body; I am not positive whether the first shot hit him in the back of the head or the breast. I stepped from behind the rig just as he fell, and Brazel got off his horse and cooly said: "This is Hell!" He handed me his revolver, and got into the buggy. I put a lap robe over the corpse, and, hitching Brazel's horse behind the buggy, we drove to Las Cruces, and Brazel surrendered, saying he killed Garrett in self defense'." [26]

On 13th April, 1908, the Dona Ana County Grand Jury listened to the presentation of evidence in the Garrett murder case. The words of Dr. W.C. Field rang in their ears as they considered the facts of the matter.

"Upon being informed of the tragedy, in company with [Deputy] Sheriff Felipe Lucero, I at once left for the scene of the killing," Dr. Field testified. "We found Garrett's body as it had fallen, undisturbed, in a six-inch sand drift beside the road. Garrett's shotgun was about four feet off to one side. There was a glove on his right hand, which naturally covered his trigger finger, but none on the left. There was a pathway in the center of the back of the head, made by a .45 calibre bullet, which had driven Garrett's long hair into the brain and had torn away the right eyebrow, unmistakable evidence, in my opinion, that he had been shot from behind.

"I later extracted another bullet that had penetrated the body from the upper part of the stomach to the upper part of the shoulders. I made careful measurements of distances and closely investigated conditions at the scene of the crime, and declare unequivocally, that, in my opinion, the shooting of Pat Garrett was murder in cold blood — murder in the first degree." [27]

The Grand Jury handed down a true bill against Wayne Brazel, but bail was granted on the advice of Governor George Curry, who believed that if Brazel was jailed pending trial it "might be a source of ill feeling among his cowpuncher friends." [28] The bail was set at $10,000 and W.W. Cox raised it in less than an hour, the bond being signed by Cox himself, George W. Freeman, B.F. Lane, J.S. Queensbury, F.H. Bascom, J.W. Taylor, Jeff D. Isaacs, Henry Stoes and J.H. May. [29] The indictment, a typically verbose legal document of the period, charged that "he, the said Wayne Brazel, did on the twenty-ninth of February, 1908, in Dona Ana County, Territory of New Mexico, with force of arms in and upon one Patrick F. Garrett, there and then with a certain pistol, loaded with gunpowder and various leaden bullets, did kill and murder the said Patrick F. Garrett."[30]

In the early fall, still hoping to raise some money to pay a detective, James M. Hervey visited another of Garrett's friends, the writer Emerson Hough.

"I went to Chicago some six or eight months after Garrett's death and contacted Hough and told him this entire story and asked him if he, alone or with some friends, would make up a thousand dollars or so to try to find out who killed Garrett, but he said Garrett owed him considerable money and that he was pretty pushed for money anyway and he couldn't do it," Hervey wrote later. "Then he made this remark: 'Jimmie, I know that outfit around the Organ Mountains and Garrett got killed for trying to find out who killed Fountain and you will get killed trying to find out who killed Garrett. I advise you to let it alone'."[31]

Hervey considered that it was good advice coming from a man who knew whereof he spoke. He decided, as he put it, 'not to be so active," but he never lost interest in the case.

Jim Miller's name was by now openly being mentioned in connection with the murder and people were trying to piece the threads together. It was generally believed that Miller had been the trigger man, though some people thought that if he had not actually done the killing he had certainly planned it. Soon it was known that there had never been any herd of cattle coming up from Mexico on 15th March; that there was no ranch in Oklahoma for them to be driven to in the fall; and that neither Miller nor Adamson had any intention of buying Wayne Brazel's goats.

The El Paso undertaker, who had hurried to Las Cruces with the longer-than-usual coffin for Garrett, told Captain John R. Hughes of the Texas Rangers that he had seen Jim Miller in Las Cruces in conversation with a man he knew to be one of Garrett's enemies.[32] Others said that Miller had been seen at Tularosa[33] and White Oaks a few days before the murder, that he had been in El Paso, too, and that on the actual day Garrett was killed he had been seen in a bank and in the Park Hotel at Las Cruces.[34]

James M. Hervey suggested to Fred Fornoff that as his job carried a limited expense account he might be able to dig up something in El Paso. Fornoff spent some time talking to people — possibly Mannie Clements among them — and returned to Santa Fe with the full story of the meeting that had been held at the St. Regis Hotel. He knew the name of the rancher who had arranged the killing, had heard Miller's fee mentioned as being $1,500 and knew that Mannie Clements had picked it up in a lawyer's office. Except in his last murder-for-pay, Jim Miller always collected at least half of his fee before he did the job in hand. Fornoff thought he knew which lawyer was involved, too. He also knew that the deal included the furnishing of a man to confess to the murder and a second man to testify that it was self-defense. The only snag was that he could prove none of his assertions. [35]

Lawman Dee Harkey also stumbled across evidence when he went out to the ranch he jointly owned with Judge Charles Brice. One of his horses was missing and he asked his foreman, Joe Beasley, where it was. Beasley said it was dead.

"Miller rode him over and killed Pat Garrett, and told me what he had done," the foreman explained. "He said that if he was ever indicted for it, he was going to expect to show by me that he was here at your ranch at the time Pat Garrett was killed." [36]

Harkey immediately told Attorney-General Hervey what his foreman had said. Beasley was a petty criminal and well-known to the law officer. He was "a notorious character," Hervey said, "always getting into small difficulties in court — gambling without a license, selling liquor to minors, and other small offences. He was always turning up as a witness for defendants in criminal cases." He immediately sent a man to talk to Beasley. [37] When the investigator returned he gave Hervey the full story.

"Beasley said that Miller came through Portales early in the morning before this killing and said he wanted a horse, that he was going to make a long ride to Las Cruces and bump off Garrett and that he must get to Fort Worth as soon as possible to have an alibi," Hervey wrote. "Beasley further reported that Miller said that when he got to Fort Worth he would send this Portales fellow a telegram so a record would be made and he could say he was in Fort Worth at the time. Miller confirmed the story that the ranchman referred to employed him to do this and was to furnish the witness and the party who would claim that he killed Garrett in self-defense." [38]

The trouble was that all this was hearsay evidence and Beasley's record was so appalling that he could never be put on the witness stand to face Fall as defending counsel. Both Hervey and Fornoff had managed to get the correct story, but neither could prove it in a court of law.

"If Captain Fornoff had been able to employ competent secret service men, I am confident he would have been able to develop the facts in this case," George Curry said later. "Attorney-General Hervey did not believe in Brazel's guilt and declined to appear for the Territory, which had my approval." [39]

One positive effect of Garrett's death was that W.W. Cox was able to get hold of his land and the water he wanted. He bought out the Garrett family and they moved away.[40]

In the summer of 1908, after four months of investigating, John Scanland was ready to publish his little book. He called it **Life of Pat F. Garrett and The Taming of the Border Outlaw** and its appearance caused immediate concern among the plotters. For Scanland, a competent reporter and investigator, did not mince his words. He was too canny to call names in every instance, but he often hinted strongly at what he either knew or suspected, and he was remarkably frank in stating his opinions in the first part of the book which dealt with Garrett's murder and the events leading up to it. He wrote about the money troubles that Garrett had been having, about his loan from Cox, of Brazel and the goats and Garrett's intention to get the Bear Canyon ranch back by legal action. He had conducted numerous interviews, including ones with Wayne Brazel and Carl Adamson, and had talked confidentially to many people who were in a position to know a great deal of detail. After stating specific facts, Scanland moved into the realm of informed speculation about the dubious events surrounding the death of the man who, he told his readers, "was personally known to more men in the Southwest than any other man in the country, and was known by reputation almost throughout the entire country."[41] He made some interesting points.

"The news of his violent death was received with consternation," Scanland wrote. "It was strange that he should be unprepared, or rather not on his guard, was the general remark, and many hinted at a plot. These hints broadened into what the friends of Garrett deemed well-grounded suspicions, when it was remembered that about a week before the tragedy, Garrett had informed George Curry, and other friends in El Paso, that he expected trouble from the very source whence it came. . .

"His shotgun was loaded with bird shot — evidence that he did not expect to use his weapon — or, rather, it was contrary to his presentiment of impending danger . . . And, stranger still, that one with his experience, and skill with a gun, should, in a quarrel, permit his antagonist to 'get the drop' on him. That he did not expect trouble at that moment is evidenced from the fact that his antagonist did 'get the drop' on him, is the belief of all who knew Garrett, and his record warrants this belief. The sworn statement of Carl Adamson, the only living witness to the tragedy except Brazel, is also corroborative in this belief. . . He further states that Garrett took his shotgun out of the buggy, and had threatened Brazel. Such men as Garrett do not make threats. They shoot first. Furthermore, had he made a threat, there was no use in him getting out of the buggy to carry it into execution — he could have shot from where he sat. Besides, he would not have partly turned his back to his antagonist, after getting out of the buggy, with his gun, and making the threat — if such was the truth!"[42]

Scanland might had added that if Garrett had planned to fight he would have taken a six-shooter along as well, even if he intended to use the shotgun, just in case. He believed that when Garrett said: "I can get you off any way," he was referring to doing it legally, as he had been told he could by the El Paso lawyer.[43]

Scanland ended his speculation with an ominous suggestion.

"There is a mystery about this tragedy, and it may never come to light," he said. "Whether there was a plot is unknown; yet, suspicions are strong that there was. It is hinted by the friends of Garrett that astounding revelations will be made."[44]

It must indeed have appeared to the plotters that there was a strong possiblity that "astounding revelations" might be made and that the whole squalid business would become public knowledge before Brazel's trial. Miller very obviously would not talk and Adamson had been convicted of smuggling Chinese into the United States across the Mexican border, so he was out the way.[45] Brazel, Fall, Cox and Lee, and presumably "Print" Rhode, were also hardly likely to run to the authorities.

Mannie Clements was the weak link, jovial Mannie, who liked his drink and social chat. There was the possibility that neither friendship nor fear would keep his lips sealed. Fall, particularly, did not like Mannie Clements and there had been bad blood between them for more than twelve years because Fall had successfully defended the man who shot Mannie's cousin John Wesley Hardin in the back.[46] Something needed to be done about Mannie, and it soon was. On 29th December, 1908, he strolled into Tom Powers' "Coney Island" Saloon in El Paso and a few minutes later he was dead. Nobody saw what happened. Barman Joe Brown, one of the three on duty, remarked to customer W.H. Fryer who arrived a few moments after the shooting: "Mannie Clements just committed suicide." Brown was subsequently arrested for the murder but came clear at his trial. Mannie was not El Paso's favorite son and it may be suspected that the authorities were rather less than vigilant in their investigations.[47] The trial was quite controversial, but how Mannie was killed and by whom never came out. There were various theories and some years later Albert B. Fall's supporter and legal associate Mark B. Thompson, in answer to a direct question as to how Clements died and who killed him, said that he did not know, but went on to suggest that it was entirely possible that when Mannie walked into the saloon and approached the bar the barman was polishing glasses. He could,

Thompson said, easily have had a gun under the polishing cloth, shot Mannie down and then dropped the gun into the bowl of suds used for the washing up.[48]

After Attorney-General Hervey withdrew from the prosecution of Wayne Brazel, the case was put into the hands of Mark Thompson, who, as Curry had remarked, "was a pretty close friend of Fall's."[49] Thompson apparently knew nothing of the conspiracy at first and subpoenaed from the Western Union Telegraph Company the batch of telegrams sent by and between Adamson, Miller, Brazel, "Print" Rhode and W.W. Cox.[50] He suddenly stopped right there and the telegrams were never produced in court. It got around locally that certain interested parties had warned the prosecutor not to dig too diligently.

Dr. W.C. Field visited Thompson and told him all that he had discovered or deduced, bravely saying that he was not afraid to testify to the fullest extent. Thompson thanked him and said that he would ask for what he wanted when he had the doctor on the stand.[51]

Brazel's trial was set for mid-April, 1909, nearly fourteen months after the murder of Pat Garrett, although it hardly seems that it need have taken nearly so long. When the trial was only a few days off news was received that Jim Miller was in trouble.

Nobody knew exactly what the difficulty was about, except that it involved another killing, as usual for money, up in the town of Ada, Oklahoma. It appeared tht Miller had shot an ex-lawman named Bobbitt, who was also a prominent Mason, and that he had not managed to get clear with his usual efficiency, having been traced to a ranch near his home in Fort Worth and there been arrested. The Texas newspapers during March were full of conflicting stories about his crime, flight and apprehension, and the fact that he had been taken back to Oklahoma to languish in the Pontotoc County jail pending a full investigation of the Bobbitt Murder. However, with Wayne Brazel's trial just around the corner, it was not considered prudent to mention Jim Miller's name too loudly around Las Cruces, and those who had an interest either in Miller's continued well-being, or speedy, silent demise, read their newspapers and kept their own counsel.

On 19th April, 1909, Wayne Brazel appeared before Judge Frank W. Parker, who ten years earlier had been the trial judge in the case of Oliver Lee and Jim Gililland on the charge brought by Pat Garrett of murdering Fountain and his son. Albert B. Fall and Herbert B. Holt appeared for the defense and Mark B. Thompson for the Territory of New Mexico.

Dr. W.C. Field testified that he had accompanied Deputy Sheriff Felipe Lucero to the scene of the killing and had found Garrett's body lying in a six-inch-deep sand drift. He said that one bullet had entered the back of the head carrying some of Garrett's long hair into the brain. It had emerged at the front and torn away the right eyebrow. The second bullet, he said, had entered the upper part of the stomach, passed through the body and lodged in the shoulders. He waited to be asked other questions which would have brought out additional descrepancies in Brazel's story, but he waited in vain. Prosecutor Thompson knew what Dr. Field could tell and he made no attempt to ask questions which would bring forth embarrassing answers.[52]

Carl Adamson, the only witness to the slaying, was not even called, although he was readily accessible.[53]

Brazel had told El Paso attorney Harris Walthall that when Garrett reached for his shotgun there was a look on his face the like of which he had never seen. It was, said Brazel, a "killer look" and he knew that he had to defend himself.[54] He was staying with Bill Isaacs during the trial and kept repeating the story over and over until he was word perfect, while Isaacs listened and nodded.

"Bill," Brazel said one day, "you don't believe a damn word of my story, do you?"

"No," said Isaacs, "but it is a good story. Keep saying it over and over and you will believe it yourself. I can't. You're no killer."[55]

When he got on the stand Brazel told the story just as he had taught it to himself. Garrett, grabbing the shotgun, had snarled: "Brazel, I want you to get them damned goats off that range; if you don't I'll make you get them off," he testified. As Garrett raised the shotgun, he said, he knew that he had to kill him and that even though Carl Adamson shouted "Don't shoot him again" as Garrett went down he was so excited that he fired a second time.[56]

At 5:20 that afternoon, with little conflicting testimony before them, the Dona Ana County jury filed in the jury room. Only fifteen minutes later they took their places in court again and announced their verdict: "Not Guilty."[57]

At W.W. Cox's ranch at Organ Gap that night there was a barbecue to celebrate Wayne Brazel's acquittal. Ranchers came from miles around and as the liquor flowed, and tongues loosened up, the gay occasion turned into a celebration over the death of Pat Garrett.[58]

At about the same moment, in the small town of Ada in Oklahoma, "Killing Jim" Miller was being taken from jail by masked vigilantes to be hanged in a barn.

NOTES
CHAPTER 5

1. **New Mexico Sentinel,** 23rd April, 1939.
2. Ibid.
3. Ibid. In those days, prior to microscopic ballistic tests, a .44 Winchester bullet, after an impact with flesh and bone, would look very similar to a .45 caliber bullet from a handgun after like treatment. It is pertinent, too, that the bullet which struck Garrett in the head emerged over the eye and continued on its way, so Dr. Field had only the bullet from the body to determine the caliber.
4. Keleher, **Fabulous Frontier,** op. cit., p. 73.
5. Scanland, op. cit., p. 1.
6. Fred Fornoff was born in Baltimore, Maryland, on 6th February, 1859, and moved to Galveston, Texas, in 1877 to engage in sawmill and lumber work. By 1879 he was working as a miner in Colorado and at a later period was involved in brickmaking at Socorro and Albuquerque, New Mexico. In 1880 he was a policeman in Albuquerque at the beginning of a long career in law enforcement. **The History of New Mexico: Its Resources and People** (Pacific States Publishing Co., Los Angeles, 1907), Volume 1, p. 196, says that he was City Marshal of the town 1891-98, but his son says it was 1894-96. In 1898 he joined Roosevelt's "Rough Riders" as a member of Troop H. After the war he served as a Deputy United States Marshal in New Mexico and in 1905 was one of the first to join the newly-formed Territorial Mounted Police. Following the resignation of Captain John J. Fullerton he assumed command of the force, effective 1st April, 1906. He held the post for many years. He was a Deputy Sheriff of Bernalillo County under Sheriff Tony Ortiz and in 1921-22 was also a Deputy United States Marshal. Later he was a Special Agent for the Federal Government and served as a Detective for the Atchison, Topeka and Santa Fe Railroad. After a long illness he died at Sheridan, Wyoming, on 26th November, 1935 — Robert N. Mullin to CR, 5th May, 1968.
7. James Madison Hervey was born at Stephenville, Texas, on 4th July, 1874. His father, Austin Flint Hervey, was a supplier of stores to the buffalo hunters at Fort Griffin, and one of his brothers, Virgil, was killed there. He graduated in law from Ann Arbor University, Michigan in 1899. He rose through various appointments to become Attorney-General of New Mexico and died in 1953.
8. James Madison Hervey, art. cit., p. 17.
9. Ibid., p. 40; George Curry, **Autobiography,** op. cit., p. 217, correctly says that two .44 shells were found, though Hervey mentions only the one which he found. Siringo, **Riata and Spurs,** op. cit., p. 216, mistakenly says that only one shell case was found, and that it was Fornoff who found it.

10. James Madison Hervey, art. cit., p. 40.
11. Ibid., p. 42.
12. George Curry, **Autobiography,** op. cit., p. 217.
13. Scanland, op. cit., p. 9.
14. It is the opinion of this writer that the mystery man Brazel met is very unlikely to have been Jim Miller, who by this time should have taken up his position where he was to murder Garrett. It seems possible, therefore, that it was W.W. Cox, having a final check-up on the arrangements.
15. El Paso **Daily Herald,** 5th March , 1908. Many people believe that there was no signed contract, merely a verbal agreement over the sale of the goats.
16. George Curry, **Autobiography,** op. cit., p. 217.
17. James Madison Hervey, art. cit., p. 40.
18. George Curry, **Autobiography,** op. cit., p.216.
19. Ibid., p. 218; Keleher, **Fabulous Frontier,** op. cit., p. 73; and Jarvis P. Garrett. op. cit., p. 41.
20. George Curry, **Autobiography,** op. cit., pp. 216-17.
21. Ibid., p. 217.
22. Ibid; also James Madison Hervey, art. cit., p. 40.
23. James Madison Hervey, art. cit., p. 40.
24. Capitan **News,** 6th March, 1908.
25. Very little is known about Scanland. He was living in El Paso when his book on Garrett was published, possibly at the St. Regis Hotel where the murder was first plotted. Certainly a J.M. Scanland was listed by the 1910 City Directory as being resident at the hotel. Many years later Scanland was writing for the Los Angeles **Times** and on 12th March, 1922, the paper carried an article by him which had some unfavorable things to say about Wyatt Earp. There were also numerous historical inaccuracies in the piece, one of them being that Earp was dead. In fact he was 75 and hale and hearty. He got on Scanland's trail with the announced intention of giving the newspaperman a sound thrashing. Film star William S. Hart, a friend of the old lawman, at once took issue with the **Times** over Scanland's article and there was an exchange of correspondence between Hart and Earp on the subject for the next five years — see Wyatt and Sarah Earp to Bill Hart, 24th March, 1922; Wyatt Earp to Bill Hart, 16th November, 1924; and Wyatt Earp to Bill Hart, 18th November, 1927, all letters in the Correspondence Collection, William S. Hart Ranch, Newall, California. When Wyatt Earp met up with Scanland in a rooming house in a run-down section of Los Angeles in 1924 he found the newspaperman old and sickly. They settled for a written retraction and apology. Scanland is believed to have died around 1925 — Robert N. Mullin to CR, 20th April and 1st May, 1968.
26. Scanland, op. cit., pp. 9-10.
27. Testimony of Dr. W.C. Field, as quoted in Hamlin, **Billy the Kid,** op. cit., pp. 314-15.
28. El Paso **Daily Herald,** 5th March, 1908.
29. Keleher, **Fabulous Frontier,** op. cit., pp. 75-76, gives the names of seven of

the bondsmen and Scanland, op. cit., p. 10, adds two more.

30. Keleher, **Fabulous Frontier**, op. cit., p. 76.

31. James Madison Hervey, art. cit., p. 41; see also Keleher, **Fabulous Frontier**, op. cit., p. 74; also Keleher **Violence in Lincoln County**, op. cit., p. 304. Siringo, **Riata and Spurs**, op. cit., p. 217, quotes a letter he received from Emerson Hough, in which an unidentified peace officer's visit was mentioned, and which gave Hough's view of the murder. Writing to Siringo from Denver, Colorado, 25th September, 1922, Hough said in part: "I talked with a lawman lately from that country who said that Jim Miller was the man who killed Garrett from ambush, although W . . . B . . . got the credit for it. Pat had no more fear of W . . . B . . . than he did of a rabbit — not Patrick!"

32. Martin, **Border Boss**, op. cit., p. 151.

33. Lorenzo D. Walters, op. cit., p. 122; also Siringo, **Riata and Spurs**, op. cit., p. 216.

34. Keleher, **Fabulous Frontier**, op. cit., p. 78.

35. James Madison Hervey, art. cit., p. 42. Smith, "Dona Ana County" Part 2, art. cit., p. 3, notes: "An unverified rumor has named the lawyer as Albert Bacon Fall and the ranchman Oliver Lee." He points out that when James Madison Hervey wrote his paper in 1953 he commented that the rancher died "recently." Smith, remarking that Cox died in 1923 and Lee in 1941, implies that Lee's was the nearest death to 1953 and so, apparently, he was the rancher as indicated by the "unverified rumor," which came from his unidentified "Private correspondence from U.S.A." He concludes, though, of the murders of Fountain and Garrett: "I doubt very much, however, that Oliver Lee had a hand in either of these assassinations, although it appears that he was intimately acquainted with the details of both." I would concur with Smith's "unverfied rumor" that the lawyer in question was Fall, but am convinced that Cox was the ranchman.

36. Harkey, **Mean as Hell**, op. cit., p. 116.

37. James Madison Hervey, art. cit., p. 42; some years later Lincoln County Historian Maurice Garland Fulton was urged by Judge Charles Brice to present the facts on the Garrett killing, and, in particular, to show the evidence that Jim Miller was the trigger man. They needed an affidavit from Joe Beasley. However, by the time they got around to seeking the material Beasley had died — Hutchinson, **Another Verdict**, op. cit., p. 9, citing a letter from Fulton. It appears that Fred Fornoff's report of his findings in the Garrett murder investigation was once in Brice's possession — Mullin, — "The Key to the Mystery of Pat Garrett," art. cit., p. 5.

38. James Madison Hervey, art. cit., p. 42.

39. George Curry, **Autobiography**, op. cit., pp. 217-18. It may be argued that, knowing that the local District Attorney was Fall's friend, it was irresponsible of Hervey to withdraw from the case.

40. El Paso **Daily Herald**, 1st December, 1908; also Jarvis P. Garrett, op. cit., p. 46.

41. Scanland, op. cit., p. 6.

42. Ibid., pp. 7-8.

43. Ibid., p. 8.

44. Ibid.

45. Keleher, **Fabulous Frontier**, op. cit., p. 77.

46. The man who killed Hardin was John Selman, one of the most dangerous men on the frontier. For an account of this man's life see Metz, **John Selman,** op. cit., and especially pp. 168-93, for Hardin's death on 19th August, 1895, and his killer's trial in February, 1896.

47. El Paso **Times**, 30th and 31st December, 1908, and 1st-4th January, 1909. Brown's arrest was reported Ibid., 12th and 13th December, 1909, and his trial — Ibid., 11th-15th May, 1909. At the trial it transpired that Mannie had other troubles than those involving Garrett's death. On the night he was killed he had been making open offers to kill Charles F. McClanny, who was involved in smuggling Chinese, and he had various other enemies. See also **Pass of the North** by C.L. Sonnichsen (Texas Western Press, El Paso, 1968), pp. 340-44.

48. George Topping, "Albert Bacon Fall," art. cit., p. 66. A misprint gives Thompson's name as Thornton. **Autobiography of a Durable Sinner** by Owen P. White (G.P. Putnam, New York, 1942), pp. 103-4, also says that this was the way it was done. White claims he was given the details by Tom Powers, but he does not name the bartender. Robert N. Mullin, who knew Joe Brown in later years, reports that "when anyone asked him about the Clements matter all they got from Joe was a cold stare from his very blue eyes" — Robert N. Mullin to CR, 20th April, 1968. On one occasion Brown said: "I didn't do it, but I know who did and he didn't get his money" — Sonnichsen, **Pass of the North,** op. cit., p. 344, quoting interview with Maury Kemp, 4th October, 1953. The fact that Mannie was killed in a saloon owned by Garrett's friend Tom Powers opens up a whole new field of speculation. It will be recalled that Powers refused to contribute to a "pot" to investigate the murder, as suggested by James M. Hervey. Judge W.D. Howe says that for many years he believed that Brown was the man who killed Mannie, but he eventually came to the conclusion that Tom Powers had done it — Sonnichsen, **Pass of the North,** op. cit., p. 344, quoting Howe's manuscript "Reminiscences of El Paso."

49. James Madison Hervey, art. cit., p. 17.

50. Keleher, **Fabulous Frontier**, op. cit., p. 76.

51. **New Mexico Sentinel,** 23rd April, 1939.

52. Ibid.

53. Keleher, **Fabulous Frontier**, op. cit., p. 77.

54. Sonnichsen, **Tularosa,** op. cit., p. 242.

55. Ibid.

56. Keleher, **Fabulous Frontier**, op. cit., p. 77.

57. Sonnichsen, **Tularosa,** op. cit., p. 244.

58. Keleher, **Fabulous Frontier**, op. cit., p. 77. Views of the trial: The trial was "a farce in every sense of the word" — Jarvis P. Garrett, op. cit., p. 45; "The

Trial was a joke in a way . . . Everybody knew Pat Garrett and there just wasn't much use to attempt to convict a man of killing him" — Bert Judia, art. cit. p. 47.

CHAPTER 6
EPILOGUE

It was just less than a year from the day that he killed Pat Garrett that Jim Miller committed his next murder-for-pay. His victim was A.A. "Gus" Bobbitt, a former Deputy United States Marshal who had made plenty of enemies during his two terms of office. In particular he had clashed with cattlemen Jesse West and Joe Allen, who eventually left Pontotoc County, Oklahoma, and returned to the Texas Panhandle swearing undying hatred for Bobbitt. In due course they found the opportunity and the finances to send Jim Miller northwards from Fort Worth on a mission of murder.

He set his plan with care, renting a room in the home of a man named Oscar Peeler, thus establishing a base from where he could not only find out about the local topography, but observe the habits of his intended victim. He liked to use relatives in his schemes, because he believed that they were less likely to talk, and visited a man named Williamson — like Carl Adamson, a relative-by-marriage — who was living near the town of Francis in Indian Territory.

On 26th February, 1909, Jim Miller ambushed "Gus" Bobbitt as he was driving home to his ranch with a wagon-load of cotton seed. He shotgunned the former lawman off the wagon, mounted his horse and rode away, heading for Williamson's ranch. There he abandoned the animal and soon afterwards jumped a freight train to Fort Worth.

Bobbitt, however, was not quite dead. He lived long enough to gasp out to his wife that he believed that West and Allen were behind the whole affair and when he died his will was found to contain a bequest of $1,000 to be spent on the pursuit, arrest and conviction of "those who will murder me." Local Masons put up half as much again and, encouraged by the aggressiveness of the "2,500 Club" — a semi-vigilante organization calling for reform and "law and order" — Ada's Chief of Police, George Culver, took the trail.

He traced the fleeing horseman's journey across country to Williamson's ranch and in panic the man implicated Oscar Peeler. Culver then went to Fort Worth but at first failed to find Miller, who was hiding out at a ranch a few miles away. It did not take Culver long to locate him, however, and on 31st March he started north with "Killing Jim" as his prisoner. Culver had learned form his investigations that B.B. Burwell, of Dalhart, Texas, had been the purse-holder in the business transactions between Miller, West and Allen and soon he, too, was in the Pontotoc County jail. On 6th April both West and Allen were arrested in

Oklahoma City and sent to Ada to join Miller and Burwell. Miller lived in high style, having his meals sent in from outside, distributing $5 tips to waiters and arranging to have rugs furnished for the floors of the cells. Oscar Peeler had been the first one to be jailed and as the weeks of his imprisonment passed he began to weaken. On 18th April he talked, spilling out a story of Jesse West's involvement as the man who paid for Miller's board and lodging and his own understanding that Burwell was to pay Miller the rest of an agreed fee after the murder of Bobbitt was effected.[1]

The "2,500 Club" went into action.

On the evening of 19th April — while Wayne Brazel was being feted in the Organ Mountains of New Mexico — three masked men went to the electric plant in Ada, took it over at gunpoint and plunged the town into darkness. At the same time another group of masked vigilantes went to the jail, surprised jailer Bob Nestor and knocked him on the head when he refused to part with the keys to the cells.

The way the old-timers tell it, Jim Miller died well.

Jesse West and Joe Allen were dragged screaming from their cell along with B.B. Burwell. Oscar Peeler, who was in a nearby cage, was ignored. "Killing Jim" took the time to dress carefully, putting on a clean white shirt and assorted dress jewelry and combing his hair. The four men were marched silently through the darkened town to the old Frisco barn, ropes were produced and a white horse kept there was pressed into service for the hanging.

Seeing that there was no chance to avoid the inevitable, Miller calmly dispensed his valuables. He asked that his ring and a diamond stud be sent to his wife in Fort Worth and handed his executioners a diamond stickpin, with instructions that it be given to a guard named McCarthy who had been good to him.

"You've got a job to do. Why don't you do it?" he demanded as the vigilantes delayed the business in hand. "Let's get this over as soon as possible." As they tied his hands behind his back and sat him astride the horse, he said: "Let there be no mistake."

There was none.

Nor was there error in the cases of Jesse West, Joe Allen or B.B. Burwell and, their work done, the vigilantes melted in the night.[2]

The identity of the mob was never made public and the bodies of the four men were sent to their respective home towns. Miller's corpse was shipped back to Fort Worth and buried by his sorrowing wife. Considering his major source of income, a fact not unknown among newspaper editors as well as potential employers of his talents, it was surprising that the prevailing Press comment was one of sadness and not of joy. The Galveston **News** even went so far as to say that "most of his victims were either cattle thieves or men whom he shot in self-defense."[3]

There were those in New Mexico who said that Jim Miller made a confession to several killings, Garrett's included, before he was strung up to a beam in the Frisco barn, and in almost every case the fee he received for the murder of Garrett was supposed to have featured in his last words.

Texas Ranger Captain John R. Hughes told friends that Miller claimed to have had $1,000 for the job.[4] The figure which had been obtained by Fred Fornoff was $1,500 and this was probably also too low. Mrs. Katherine Doughty Stoes of Las Cruces heard that Miller said his fee had been $2,000.[5] A range man, who knew Cox well and believed that he had been the man who hired Miller, was told by George Curry that the fee paid was $5,000,[6] and this is most probably the correct sum, though the figure will undoubtedly always be in dispute because of the very nature of the transaction.

Lorenzo D. Walters, who had known Wayne Brazel at the turn of the century, thought him somewhat ponderous, and also believed that Garrett was one of the quickest men with a gun in the entire Southwest, commented sarcastically of the self-confessed killer: "He must have surely picked up some speed to have beat Pat Garrett to the draw." The murder of Garrett, he said, was "a frame up by his enemies" and the way that Walters heard it, Miller got $10,000 for the job, but there was a nice twist in his version: Miller did not have time to collect the money before departing for Oklahoma to kill "Gus" Bobbitt, and as he got lynched there his employers in the Garrett case pocketed their money, having had the job done for free.[7] It was a good story, even though untrue.

All the figures — with the possible exceptions of the ones obtained by Fornoff and Curry — are, of course, mere guesswork. For Jim Miller, like the other gun-for-hire Tom Horn,[8] legally hanged only six years earlier, went to the grave with his lips sealed and with no trusts betrayed.[9]

The murder of Pat Garrett was never cleared up to the satisfaction of anyone — apart from those who had a direct hand in it.

One of the people who undoubtedly knew the truth was Herbert B. Holt, who, with Albert B. Fall, defended Wayne Brazel at his trial.

"I got him off the Garrett killing on self-defense, but I knew he didn't do it," Holt — seemingly forgetting that he was only junior counsel to Fall — said years later. "Jim Miller killed Pat Garrett."[10]

Harry N. Bailey, who had had real estate dealings with Garrett and was in Las Cruces on the afternoon of the murder, called the whole affair "a clean-cut job which was put up to murder him."[11]

Captain John R. Hughes never believed that his old friend Garrett was killed by Brazel. The Ranger's suspicions were aroused when the man who took the coffin to Las Cruces told Hughes that he had seen Miller talking to one of Garrett's enemies. After that the lawman sniffed around a bit. He made no formal investigation because the affair was out of his domain, but he told his biographer, Jack Martin, that, basing his statement on "unimpeachable sources," he had concluded "that Garrett was 'put on the spot' and assassinated by a professional killer." He believed that man to have been Jim Miller, but conceded that if Miller did not actually fire the fatal shot he was the one who made the arrangements and that he "was close at hand when Garrett breathed his last."[12] James B. Gillett,[13] another oldtime Texas Ranger, shared Hughes' view.[14]

Judge Charles Brice, who knew a great deal about Miller, believed the story that his ranch foreman, Joe Beasley, told him about Miller having taken a horse and ridden it to death in getting away from the scene of the crime. "There is no question but what Jim Miller did the killing, and rode our horse down to do it," the jurist said many years later. "Tom Coggins always went his bond, and I did him a favor once and he wanted to pay me. I told him all I asked was to tell me who killed Pat Garrett, so he told me the whole story."[15] Judge Brice thought the case comparable with the murder-for-pay that Jim Miller committed in Collingsworth County, Texas, and to which Lawrence Angel confessed.

The fact that eye-witness Carl Adamson did not appear at the trial was something that people found most unsatisfactory.

"The case is over and done with, but some of us old-timers still have our doubts of the way justice worked out," said pioneer newspaperman Allen Pape. "We can't help but wonder why Adamson, the only eye-witness to the killing, was never put under bond, but allowed to melt out of sight before he could give his testimony to the jury."[16]

Adamson's absence at the trial, and the way nobody got around to talking about calling him, becomes all the more strange in view of the fact that he was at that very time easily accessible, as he was trying to appeal against sentence for smuggling Chinese.[17] He subsequently died of typhoid fever.[18]

And the known pacifism of Wayne Brazel caused considerable comment.

"Nobody who knew Brazel believed that he had fired those shots," said Bert Judia. "Whoever did so was a much better marksman than Wayne, and the killer was unhampered by a horse that went loco when a gun was fired. He was also unhampered by a heavy coat buttoned about him. Wayne couldn't have done it — it just wasn't physically possible." Judia believed that he was "just incapable of killing, especially in cold blood."[19]

Why, then, did Wayne Brazel take the blame for a crime he did not commit?

"I believe that he feared for his life if he told the facts," said George Curry.[20]

Undoubtedly he was right up to a point, for if Brazel had talked he would certainly have died suddenly and unexpectedly, would have died even if he had shown signs of weakening in his determination to tell the story that had been agreed, but that does not answer what made Brazel enter into the conspiracy, with his eyes wide open, in the beginning.

Western writer Hoffman Birney believed the motive was money and heard that Brazel got $1,500 for taking the blame for Garrett's death.[21]

Others thought that he took no money and was the front man just because it was asked of him.

"Wayne Brazel was always Cox's man Friday, worked for Cox about all the time," commented one old range man who knew Cox, liked him and did business with him, and so came to know the place and most of the circumstances. "I don't think he got any money out of it. Brazel just done what Cox told him to do. This was a carefully laid plot and it worked out to perfection."[22]

There were also theories about the murder, theories which cleared Jim Miller, though not many people believed them.

Bill Isaacs, who had had a good opportunity to observe Brazel during the trial, believed that Carl Adamson had done the actual shooting. He thought it probable that Brazel carried a rifle and pistol that fateful morning, but that the pistol was Adamson's, the two men having swapped guns the day before. He believed that when Garrett got down to relieve himself Adamson shot him through the body with Brazel's pistol, but that did not account for the shot in the head. Jarvis P. Garrett returned to New Mexico from South America shortly after World War II and Bill Isaacs took him out along the Las Cruces road one day to show him the little round stone he had placed on the spot where Garrett died all those years before. He told his theory to Jarvis Garrett, who accepted it.[23]

Another version of the story claimed that W.W. Cox himself killed Pat Garrett. The way this one was told, Wayne Brazel was horrified to see Cox, whom he idolized, rear up from behind a bush and pump a shot into Garrett. In order to take the heat off Cox, Wayne Brazel, the ultra-loyal cowboy, turned himself in and took the blame for the crime.[24]

Those who whispered about W.W. Cox did so very discreetly, for the counsel which Emerson Hough had given Jim Hervey was good. There was no point in getting killed for making too much noise about who might or might not have murdered Pat Garrett, or why. People muttered about Oliver Lee and Albert Bacon Fall, too, but even more softly.

Cox, having bought Garrett's ranch, had gained the water he wanted so badly and he went on to raise a fine family, to become prominent in business and banking circles in Las Cruces and to die full of years of memories on 23rd December, 1923. [25]

Fall went from strength to strength in politics. He became a Senator in the State Legislature and then in 1912 the first Senator from New Mexico to be elected to the United States Senate. He was re-elected in 1918 and became Secretary of the Interior in President Warren G. Harding's cabinet. Just two years later he resigned and until 1931 fought a losing battle against charges that he had taken a huge bribe in connection with oil leases in Wyoming. The case became nationally known as the Teapot Dome Scandal. The man who defended Fall in court was, significantly, Mark B. Thompson — who had handled the half-hearted prosecution of Wayne Brazel for the murder of Pat Garrett. Fall finally went to prison and died at the age of 88, broken in health, and perhaps in spirit, in El Paso on 30th November, 1944. [26]

Oliver Lee also became a pillar of the community and a Senator in the New Mexico State Legislature. He was salty to the very end — those who knew him well said he carried a gun even in the halls of the Legislature — and died in Alamogordo on 15th December, 1941, a distinguished and useful citizen of the State where he had spent fifty-seven years of his life. [27]

After the trial and the barbecue at W.W. Cox's ranch, Wayne Brazel gradually dropped from the public eye in New Mexico. He was occasionally pointed out to strangers as "the man who killed Pat Garrett" — and if Jim Miller had lived, wagging tongues would no doubt have kept the controversy alive — but with "Killing Jim" in his grave in Fort Worth, and with Mannie Clements, who undoubtedly knew too much for his own longevity, also gone, the matter slipped into obscurity, along with the Fountain affair with which it certainly had some connection. Most of those who knew the truth about either killing, or both, had blood or emotional ties which sealed lips. A handful of people who were neither kith nor kin, and were in possession of potentially dangerous information, "kept still," as the range country parlance has it, through fear.

Wayne Brazel never publicly denied that he had killed Pat Garrett, sticking carefully to his story of the events on the Las Cruces road until he eventually dropped from sight. Some years later, while ranching near Lordsburg, New Mexico, he allegedly confided to J.R. Galusha: "I didn't kill Pat Garrett. I just took the rap for Jim Miller." [28] Ernest Houghton Mathews of Roswell once said that Brazel told another Roswell citizen pretty much the same thing. [29] Other men who knew Brazel well staunchly maintain that such a confession to perjury would have been completely out of character. Some of the present generation of Brazels are convinced that Wayne fired the fatal shots, that he did so in the heat of the moment to protect himself, that he was not involved in any kind of murder plot and that he acted just as he said he did in court.[30]

In 1913, after making a statement connected with a homestead claim which became a matter of contention, he was accused of forgery, but in November the following year the Assistant United States District Attorney at Santa Fe asked the Federal Court to dismiss the charge for "lack of evidence."[31] Wayne Brazel's movements after 1914 are unknown, although it is believed that he went first to Lordsburg, New Mexico, and then to Arizona and finally elsewhere. Not even his brother Rothmer, or the brother and sister of Wayne's wife, know where or when he died.[32]

He covered his tracks well.

G.I. Scott of Phoenix, Arizona, worked with Wayne Brazel's son in 1961 but never learned anything about the father. He was told by old-time Arizona lawman "Buster" Brown that Wayne got into trouble in Arizona and moved to Nebraska, assuming another name and dying in that State in 1950.[33] The only thing that is certain is that he did not, as James Madison Hervey was told, expire "suddenly of a heart attack" not long after the Garrett murder trial.[34]

So, apparently, died the man who said he killed Pat Garrett, some forty-odd years after the deed and in total obscurity.

If the trial for his alleged crime had been prosecuted with verve, initiative and forcefulness could he have been convicted? Would it have led to other killing as the truth came out — or to prevent it from coming out? These are questions that the last of the old-time New Mexicans like to argue about on sunlit porches in the winter of their days.

Dr. W.C. Field, who had examined Garrett's body, and had wanted to testify that he had been murdered in cold blood if not worse, summed up the whole case with the shrewdness of a man who had lived out his life among range men.

"I never gave that testimony in detail, because I wasn't asked," he said. "Would it have made any difference in the verdict which acquitted Wayne Brazel? Who can tell? Pat had lost his money, he'd lost many of his powerful friends. These circumstances are sometimes just as important as a country doctor's testimony."[35]

NOTES
CHAPTER 6

1. There are various accounts of the crime which Miller committed and of his lynching. Most of my version comes from Perry J. Sherman of Corpus Christi, Texas. Sherman was in Ada at the time, his father being a prominent contractor there, and knew not only the circumstances but also many of the participating members of the "2,500 Club" — Sherman to CR, 18th July, 1960; see also Keleher, **Fabulous Frontier**, op. cit., pp. 81-82; Harkey, **Mean As Hell**, op. cit., p. 117; and Sonnichsen, **Tularosa**, op. cit., p. 241; also Ada **Evening News, 19th April, 1909.**

2. **Perry J. Sherman to CR, as cited; also Ada Evening News,** op. cit. The account of Miller's last crime given by Siringo, **Riata and Spurs,** op. cit., pp. 217-18, is garbled in the extreme. He says that Jesse West was innocent and was hanged because "he was caught in bad company." The name of Gus Bobbitt is given as "Bob Gossett" and the killing is wrongly said to have been done with a pistol.

3. Galveston **News,** 20th April, 1909.

4. Martin, **Border Boss,** op. cit., p. 151.

5. Sonnichsen, **Tularosa,** op. cit., p. 241, quoting manuscript by Mrs. K.D. Stoes of Las Cruces.

6. Hutchinson, **Another Verdict,** op. cit., p. 12. His source, the "Cowman," wrote: "Many years ago Curry told me that W.W. Cox gave Miller $5,000 to do the job." He adds that Miller's name was the only one mentioned and that Curry "did not implicate anyone else." The fee of $5,000 was also the one arrived at by Western writer Hoffman Birney, who carried out an on-the-spot investigation in the late 1940s — J.C. Cykes, op. cit., pp. xv-xvi, citing Birney. My own investigation leads me to believe that this is the correct figure.

7. Lorenzo D. Walters, op. cit., pp. 121-22. He gives his source as "a well known rancher of New Mexico." Jarvis P. Garrett, op. cit., p. 45, also says that Miller did not have time to collect and gives the amount as $10,000. This figure is probably at least twice the correct one — and with the exception of his last "job," Miller always collected at least half of his fee before he killed. Siringo gives the same version, p. 217. It is fair to point out that the chapter on Garrett's murder does not appear in the first edition of Siringo's book, which was published in 1927. Lorenzo Walter's book was published in 1928 and it seems reasonable to suppose that Siringo "lifted" this piece of mis-information from it and put it in his own second edition which appeared in 1931.

8. Tom Horn was an Apache scout, Pinkerton dectective, packer in Cuba during the Spanish-American War of 1898, stock detective in Wyoming and was known to have taken on assignments to kill rustlers for money. He

finally killed a 15-year-old boy, or so it was said, though there is considerable room for doubt. He was executed in Cheyenne, Wyoming, on 23rd November, 1903 — see **The Life of Tom Horn** by Himself (privately issued by John C. Coble, printed by the Loutham Book Company, Denver, 1904; reprinted University of Oklahoma Press, Norman, 1964); **The Saga of Tom Horn** by Dean Krakel (Laramie, Wyoming, 1954); and **the Legend of Tom Horn** by Jay Monaghan (Bobbs-Merrill, Indianapolis, 1946). There are also several sketches of his life — "The Execution of Tom Horn" by Dean Krakel (Denver Westerners' **Roundup,** Volume XI, Number 6, June, 1955), pp. 5-7; Cunningham, **Triggernometry,** op. cit., as Chapter Sixteen entitled "Railroaded?"; and Coolidge, **Fighting Men of the West,** op. cit., as Chapter Four.

9. Perry J. Sherman to CR, as cited; also Sonnichsen, **Tularosa,** op. cit., p. 241, and p. 230, quoting an interview with Moss Wimbish of Ada, 4th December, 1953.

10. Judge James B. McGhee, interview with CR at Santa Fe, 9th October, 1967.

11. **When New Mexico Was Young** by Harry N. Bailey **(Las Cruces Citizen,** Las Cruces, 1948), p. 196.

12. Martin, **Border Boss,** op. cit., p. 150-51,.

13. James Buchanan Gillett was born on 4th November, 1856, at Austin, Texas, and joined the Frontier Battalion of the Texas Rangers in 1875. During his service he was involved to a greater or lesser extent in some of Texas' most famous clashes, including the Mason County War, the hunt for Sam Bass, the Horrell-Higgins Feud and the El Paso Salt War troubles. He quit with the rank of Sergeant in 1881 — and subsequently wrote a book called **Six Years with the Texas Rangers** (Yale University Press, New Haven and London, 1925; reprinted 1963). After a varied career as a railroad detective, county sheriff, city marshal of El Paso and Deputy United States Marshal, he settled down to ranching, first at Marfa and later at Alpine, Texas. Subsequently he had a ranch at Roswell, New Mexico, but sold out in 1907 to return to Marfa. He was the subject of a biographical sketch in Cunningham, **Triggernometry,** op. cit., pp. 189-202, as Chapter Seven entitled "Behind the Star." He died at Temple, Texas, on 11th June, 1937.

14. Hutchinson, **Another Verdict,** op. cit., p. 16, quoting a letter from Eugene Cunningham.

15. Judge Brice made these comments in a private letter, a copy of which was retained by his daughter, Mrs. Evelyn B. Dowaliby, of Roswell, New Mexico. Either Miller dressed up the story for Tom Coggins, or Coggins dressed it up for Judge Brice, because the way it came out was that Garrett had seen Miller and realized what was happening. "Pat had a gun down in the bottom of the buggy by his foot and got it and almost killed Miller. He said Miller said it was the closest call he ever had in any of his killings." According to Judge Brice's memory, and the old gentleman was nearly ninety at the time, "an old rancher named May had employed Miller to do this killing" — an apparent case of confusion. The only man named May who is

known to have been even remotely connected with the Miller-Brazel-Garrett affair was J.H. May who was one of Brazel's bondsmen. Judge Brice told pretty much the same story, and was adamant that Miller was the trigger man, in another private letter — Judge Brice, Roswell, to Allan A. Erwin, 31st May, 1957 — Allan A. Erwin, Desert Hot Springs, California, to CR, 12th May, 1965. It is stretching the point to say that in Miller's cases "Tom Coggins always went his bond," but he certainly helped him out on several occasions. He and Jenks Clark filled the vacuum created by Barney Riggs' killing of John Denstona and Bill Earheart. Keleher, **Fabulous Frontier,** op. cit., p. 80, notes that they "were frequently Jim Miller's sureties on appearance bonds when he was in trouble." They were both in the lobby of the Westbrook Hotel in Fort Worth when he killed Frank Fore in the lavatory in 1904. Not only did they go his bond, but actually swore at the trial that they had been eye-witnesses to the murder — Harkey, **Mean As Hell,** op. cit., p. 116.

16. Allen Pape, quoted in **Pat Garrett** by Richard O'Connor (Doubleday, New York, 1960), p. 273. The knowledgeable Robert N. Mullin is undoubtedly correct when he says: "It occured to a good many people that Adamson's testimony or the disclosure of Captain Fornoff's findings might have opened the lid of a Pandora Box" — Mullin, "The Key to the Mystery of Pat Garrett," art. cit., p. 4.

17. Carl Adamson was indicted in the Sixth Judical District of the Territory of New Mexico on a Federal complaint that on 18th June, 1908, he "unlawfully, feloniously, knowingly, wickedly, falsely, and corruptly, conspired, combined, confederated and agreed, to and with various divers persons" to smuggle Chinese into the United States. He pleaded not guilty, but was convicted at his trial in Alamogordo. He was sentenced on 14th December, 1908, to serve a year-and-a-half in prison. An appeal to the Supreme Court of the United States was never perfected — Keleher, **Fabulous Frontier,** op. cit., pp. 77-78. Keleher tells an amusing story to the effect that cowpuncher Allen Hightower, on hearing that Adamson was found guilty of trying to smuggle a wagon load of Chinese into the country, remarked: "Hell, I'd rather be caught trying to steal a wagon load of calves, than to get caught smuggling in a load of Chinese. It would be a damn sight more respectable."

18. James Madison Hervey, art. cit., p. 42.

19. Bert Judia, art. cit., p. 47.

20. George Curry, **Autobiography,** op. cit., p. 218.

21. J.C. Dykes, op. cit., pp. xv-xvi, quoting a letter from Hoffman Birney dated 2nd February, 1954.

22. Hutchinson, **Another Verdict,** op. cit., p. 12, quoting his source the "Cowman." Oliver, "Foot-Loose and Fancy Free," art. cit. p. 5, comments on Brazel's guilt thus: "In my opinion he just took the rap for the killing."

23. Jarvis P. Garrett, op. cit., p. 47; also Sonnichsen, **Tularosa,** op. cit., p.230, quoting an interview with Bill Isaacs on 15th September, 1954; and Hoffman Birney to J.C. Dykes, op. cit., pp. xv-xvi. Eugene Cunningham, who

investigated the murder and knew most of Garrett's friends and enemies in the area, did not accept Isaac's theory — Hutchinson, **Another Verdict,** op. cit., p. 16, quoting a letter from Cunningham. Adamson's descendants do not accept it either, laying the actual killing or responsiblity for arranging it, at the door of W.W. Cox for various reasons, not the least of them being the shock-induced miscarriage of Mrs. Cox following the Reed killing at the San Augustine ranch in 1899 — Phil Cooke, Santa Fe, to CR, 14th February, 1969. **Burs Under the Saddle** by Ramon F. Adams (University of Oklahoma Press, Norman, 1964), p. 122, notes: "Wayne Brazel was tried for it [Garrett's murder] though some think he assumed the blame for Carl Adamson. . ."

24. Several people have mentioned this version, but have asked that their names be witheld. Adams, op. cit., p. 220 remarks: "Many people think Jim Miller did the actual killing of Garrett although Brazel was tried for it. Of late years there seems to be some evidence that a member of the Cox family might be implicated." Fred Mazzulla, noted lawyer, Westerner and collector of frontier photographs, has in his Americana collection some unpublished material on the Garrett killing. It was described as "information about the true killer of Pat Garrett, information which indicated that Garrett was killed neither by Brazel, who was tried, nor Miller, who was hanged later for another crime. He is keeping very quiet about just who DID do it." — **The Southwesterner** (Columbus, N.M.), August, 1962. It is not known whether this indicated Adamson, Cox or some other person as the killer. Mr. Mazzulla received his information from the late W.T. Moyers, an attorney who practised law in New Mexico and "spent about 20 years digging into the real truth about Garrett." He subsequently shared an office with Fred Mazzulla and bequeathed to him the notes he had made on the Garrett murder with the proviso that his friend "promise that I would not pass the secret on to any other writer. He insisted that I write the story myself and that I sell it for a good stiff price." Mr. Mazzulla has now written up the material and says: "I believe that I am the only person who knows the story." The "good stiff price" he is asking for it is $5,000 — Fred M. Mazzulla, Denver, Colorado, to CR, 27th February, 1968. Smith, "Dona Ana County," Part 2, art. cit., p. 3, citing "Private Correspondence from U.S.A.," makes mention of the story that Cox himself did the killing when he writes; "One other story says that neither Brazel, Adamson nor Miller did the shooting — that the real killer's name has never been publicly mentioned in this connection." Smith quotes an old-timer who knew Brazel "well" as saying: "I feel quite certain that Wayne Brazel. . . told the Court that he did the shooting out of a mistaken sense of loyalty to the man who pulled the trigger; he took the blame merely to protect a man who could ill-afford to take chances with a jury." Oliver Lee had faced numerous juries and so, presumably, would not fit this description. W.W. Cox, on the other hand, would undoubtedly have been seriously embarrassed by any court action which, whether he came clear or not, would have drawn the unwelcome attentions of the Texas authorities to his whereabouts only a

few years after indictments relating to the Sutton-Taylor feud had been revived.

25. Keleher, **Fabulous Frontier,** op. cit., (1962 edition), p. 94.
26. "Albert B. Fall and the Teapot Dome Affair" by David H. Stratton (Unpublished Ph.D. dissertation, University of Colorado, Denver, 1955); **The Teapot Dome Scandal** by M.R. Werner and John Starr (Cassell, London, 1961); Keleher, **Fabulous Frontier,** op. cit., p. 201, provides a formidable list of materials and court cases relating to the affair.
27. Keleher, **Fabulous Frontier,** op. cit., p. 211.
28. "Off the Beaten Path" by Howard Bryan, **Albuquerque Tribune,** 1st March, 1968, in an article run to coincide with the sixtieth anniversary of Garrett's murder. Galusha had been a member of the Territorial Mounted Police in 1909, serving under Captain Fred Fornoff, and was later a Deputy United States Marshal.
29. In a letter to Southwestern historian Philip J. Rasch dated 2nd/3rd March, 1956, Ernest Houston Mathews — who believed that Garrett was killed "because he was causing Lee too much trouble" — remarked: "According to John Meadows, Brazil (sic) told Charles Whiteman of Roswell that he did not kill Garrett . . . " — Philip J. Rasch, Jacksonville, North Carolina, to William R. Smith, 29th January, 1966, quoted in Smith, "Dona Ana County," Part 1, art. cit., p. 12. The American critic "Quago," when reviewing O'Connor, **Pat Garrett,** op. cit., said that the author was mistaken in his assertion that Brazel stuck to his story — (English Westerners' **Tally Sheet,** Volume VI, Number 6, September-October, 1960), pp. 25-27 — but when queried was unable to provide chapter and verse, except to say that he had seen this reported in both the Silver City and Santa Fe newspapers. Smith followed this line, but without success.
30. Robert N. Mullin to CR, 1st April, 1965.
31. Santa Fe **New Mexican,** 11th November, 1914. Smith, "Dona Ana County," Part 1, art. cit., p. 12, reports that the Federal Records Center at Denver, Colorado advised him that "the documents in this case make no reference to Pat Garrett" — E.H. Pubols to William R. Smith, 6th December, 1966.
32. Robert N. Mullin to CR, 1st April, 1965. Mr. Mullin writes: "On and off over the years I've followed literally dozens of blind trails in the search but his whereabouts in 1914 is the end of the road for me." A story to the effect that Brazel went to South America and was killed there by a man named Dey is believed by several old-timers who had known Brazel personally in New Mexico — William R. Smith, Liverpool, to CR, 22nd February, 1968. The man Dey referred to is supposed to have been a former member of Butch Cassidy's "Wild Bunch." There is some evidence that when Cassidy and Harry Longabaugh robbed the bank at Mercedes, in the Province of San Luis, Republic of Argentina, in March, 1906, they were aided by a man named Dey, an American fugitive. They stole $20,000 and one of them killed a bank employee — **The Outlaw Trail; A History of Butch Cassidy and his Wild Bunch** by Charles Kelly (Devin-Adair, New York, 1959), p. 289. After the

divison of loot Dey went to Bolivia and while staying at an hotel met a Dr. Lovelace from Texas. The doctor saw Dey's bag, which was filled with gold coins, and commented upon the wealth, to which Dey is supposed to have replied: "The Lord has treated me very generously lately." — **Desperate Men** by James D. Horan (Transworld Publishers, London, 1956), p. 366, apparently quoting from the New York **Herald,** 23rd September, 1906. Horan tells the same story in **The Wild Bunch** (New American Library, New York, 1958), pp. 158-59. In **A Pictorial History of the Wild West** by Horan and Paul Sann (Arco, London, 1955), p. 231, the figure for the money stolen is given as $10,000. Dey, according to the authors, subsequently returned to the United States, though no date is given. Apparently he was careless with his luggage again, as a clergyman who was a fellow passenger on the New York-bound ship happened to see the gold in his baggage and, like Lovelace, commented on it. Dey replied "Ah, yes, Reverend, the Lord has been uncommonly good to me lately" — Ibid., p. 237, quoting the New York **World** as the source. It is possible, though in my opinion unlikely, that Brazel was killed by Dey in South America.

33. Editor's Note in **True West** (Austin, Texas, Volume 9, Number 2, Whole Number 48, November-December, 1961), p. 46. Scott was told that Wayne, by this time a widower, re-married in Nebraska.

34. James Madison Hervey, art. cit., p. 42.

35. **New Mexico Sentinel,** 23rd April, 1939.

BIBLIOGRAPHY

Adams, Ramon F. **Burs Under the Saddle.** Norman: University of Oklahoma Press, 1964.

Cline, Donald. **Alias Billy the Kid: The Man Behind the Legend.** Santa Fe, NM: Sunstone Press, 1986.

Curry George, **George Curry, 1861-1947, An Autobiography.** Edited by H.B. Henning.. Albuquerque: University of New Mexico Press, 1958.

Dykes, Jefferson C. **Law on a Wild Frontier; Four Sheriffs of Lincoln County.** Washington, DC: Potomac Corral, The Westerners, 1969.

Garrett, Patrick Floyd. **The Authentic Life of Billy the Kid,** Norman, OK: University of Oklahoma, 1954.

Gibson, A.M. **The Life and Death of Colonel Albert Jennings Fountain.** Norman: University of Oklahoma, 1965.

Hall, Ruth K. **A Place of Her Own: The Story of Elizabeth Garrett.** Rev. ed. Santa Fe, NM: Sunstone Press, 1983.

Hertzog, Peter. **Outlaws of New Mexico.** Santa Fe, NM: Sunstone Press, 1984.

Hutchinson, W.H., **Another Verdict for Oliver Lee.** Clarendon, TX: Clarendon Press, 1965.

_____, **A Bar Cross Man: The Life and Personal Writings of Eugene Manlove Rhodes.** Norman: University of Oklahoma, 1956.

Keleher, William A. **The Fabulous Frontier: Twelve New Mexico Items.** Santa Fe, NM: Rydal Press, 1945.

_____. _____. Albuquerque, NM: University of New Mexico Press, 1962.

_____. **Violence in Lincoln County, 1869-1881.** Albuquerque, NM: University of New Mexico Press, 1957.

Metz, Leon C. **Pat Garrett, The Story of a Western Lawman.** Norman, OK: University of Oklahoma, 1973.

O'Connor, Richard. **Pat Garrett.** New York: Doubleday, 1960.

Poe, John W. **The True Story of the Killing of Billy the Kid, as told to E.A. Brininstool.** Houston: Frontier Press, 1958.

Scanland, John Milton. **Life of Pat Garrett and the Taming of The Border Outlaw.** El Paso, TX: Hodge, 1908.

_____. _____. El Paso, TX: Southwestern, 1952.

Siringo, Charles A. **Riata and Spurs.** Boston: Houghton Mifflin, 1931.

Sonnichsen, C.L. **Tularosa: Last of the Frontier West.** New York: Devin-Adair, 1961.

_____. _____. Rev. ed. Albuquerque: University of New Mexico Press, 1980.

INDEX